Notker Wolf
with Leo G. Linder

Aging
Starts
in Your
Mind

You're only as old as you feel

Translated by Gerlinde Büchinger-Schmid

PARACLETE PRESS
BREWSTER, MASSACHUSETTS

2017 First Printing in English

Aging Starts in Your Mind: You're Only as Old as You Feel

English Translation Copyright © 2017 by Gerlinde Büchinger-Schmid
Edited by Sue Bollans
Original title: *Altwerden beginnt im Kopf—Jungbleiben auch* by Abtprimas Notker Wolf with Leo G. Linder © 2015 by adeo Verlag in der Gerth Medien GmbH, Asslar, Germany.

ISBN 978-1-61261-814-2

The Paraclete Press name and logo (dove on cross) are trademarks of Paraclete Press, Inc.

Library of Congress Cataloging-in-Publication Data

Names: Wolf, Notker, author.
Title: Aging starts in your mind : you're only as old as you feel / by Notker
  Wolf, with Leo G. Linder ; translated by Gerlinde Buechinger-Schmid.
Other titles: Altwerden beginnt im Kopf—Jungbleiben auch. English
Description: Brewster, Massachusetts : Paraclete Press, Inc., 2017.
Identifiers: LCCN 2017010321 | ISBN 9781612618142 (trade pbk.)
Subjects: LCSH: Aging. | Older people. | Conduct of life.
Classification: LCC HQ1061 .W597 2017 | DDC 305.26—dc23
LC record available at https://lccn.loc.gov/2017010321

10 9 8 7 6 5 4 3 2 1

Published by Paraclete Press
Brewster, Massachusetts
www.paracletepress.com

Printed in the United States of America

You're only as old as you feel

ABBOT PRIMATE NOTKER WOLF

Abbot Primate Notker Wolf was born in 1940. He studied philosophy, theology, zoology, inorganic chemistry, and the history of astronomy and holds the title Doctor of Philosophy. In 2000 he was elected abbot primate, the highest representative of the Benedictine order. He is the worldwide spokesman for Christianity's oldest order that has 7,500 monks and 17,100 nuns.

LEO G. LINDER

Leo G. Linder was born in 1948. After a period in the navy, from 1972 onward he studied film and philosophy at the Academy of Art in Düsseldorf and history and Spanish at Düsseldorf University. From 1977, he worked as a cameraman and in 1985 changed to direction, making numerous documentary films. Since 1990 he has published forty five books on topics such as theology, history, and politics. The author and director lives in Düsseldorf.

Notker Wolf gives us the courage to accept old age not only with all its advantages and accumulated experience, but also with its physical limitations. For him what counts is the way we see things.

Contents

1.

Ciao, Bella!

The older I get, the more I find it difficult to take the world seriously. Close up, it can appear merciless, almost threatening. But with increasing distance, it is looking more and more comical to me. When this happens, I pull on my pipe, grin to myself, and think, *Go on. Try to impress me. Take a tumble; I'll watch.* I admit, I sometimes enjoy the spectacle. Of course I'm to blame when I don't keep my mouth shut. But I blame my increasing age too.

I'm not the only one who feels like this. Years ago, I was invited by the then–Federal President of Germany Roman Herzog to accompany him on a trip to Korea. Once during our journey, I sat next to him on the bus. Herzog was in his midsixties, and I asked, "Mr. President, what will you do when your term has ended? What are your plans?"

"Pursuing my favorite pastime, which I'm unfortunately prevented from doing at the moment," he replied.

I looked at him. "Yes, and what would that be?"

"Poking fun."

I laughed. "Then we both have the same weakness—or strength."

I felt sorry for him; how awful to have to keep your mouth shut because of your job.

It's strange. As your own situation becomes more serious—after all, I'm now approaching seventy-five—the world becomes more of a source of amusement. My overanxious, high-and-mighty contemporaries, for example. This is nothing new for me. Directness and mild mischievousness have always been a few of the benefits of Benedictine independence. Over the years, however, my inner freedom has grown.

This freedom is a beautiful gift of old age. But perhaps the desire to poke fun is just a transitional stage. I can't yet call myself "really old." Maybe someday I'll achieve that truly endearing good humor that makes old people so thoroughly enjoyable. I'm reminded of two very old women I met by chance one day in an Italian mountain village.

On the way to the rectory, I turned down a small lane, and there they sat in cozy togetherness on a gnarled bench, backs against the side of a house and blinking into the late afternoon sun. I had hardly reached them when they perked up and boldly seized the opportunity to chat with a stranger. They wanted to know where I came from, what had brought me to their village, and all kinds of other things.

They were so delighted with this unexpected distraction that they asked a long string of questions. I responded with amusement, we chatted and joked, and then one of them asked me with a mischievous smile, "Can you guess how old Elisabetta is?"

It was difficult to say; Elisabetta could have been seventy or a hundred. So I shook my head and guessed, "Just past seventy-five?" I was hopelessly wrong.

"What do you mean?" the questioner rebuked me with mock indignation. "Ninety-two."

Elisabetta added, wagging her finger, "Plus two months."

We laughed. I sincerely complimented Elisabetta on how well she looked for ninety-two and promised to come by again on her hundredth birthday.

I continued on my way with a smile. Lovable old people like these are the purest and most delightful examples of our species. How easy and pleasant it is to have a warmhearted and humorous conversation with them, free of any egotism and ulterior motives. They no longer ask much of life—they've became modest and undemanding and seem liberated for just that reason. Liberated from wishes and desires, from greed and craving for life.

Having had so many jolts from life, having so often been delighted and so often disappointed, they've learned one thing above all others: to take life as it comes. Not to resist, not to rebel, not to have objections to their own fate. The rules of the world have lost validity for them; they no longer feel the need to intervene; they've long since withdrawn, and this gradual leave-taking has released in them a guileless, downright sunny humor. So they are one step ahead of me.

The ninety-two-year-old Elisabetta acknowledged my compliment with a smile touched by a little justified pride mixed with a slight melancholy. Are pride and melancholy the crucial ingredients of the kind of humor that, if we are lucky, old age brings? Let's look at a figure I particularly treasure, on the stage of everyday life: the elderly Roman woman.

Elderly Roman women take care of themselves. They don't go out without putting on their makeup, doing their hair, and putting on jewelry. They are ladies; they want to be seen and noticed, and they move accordingly, with a steady gate and heads held high. They have style, and style always goes down well in Rome.

One of these old ladies comes into the market when I am shopping. In all her finery and beauty, she first has a long chat with the owner. He's probably heard all her stories before, but man does not live by bread alone, and before the main performance there must be an overture. She proceeds to assemble her purchases with great care and connoisseurship.

The bacon is tried, the cheese felt, the honeydew melon sniffed; everything is selected piece by piece as if it were a treasure. A spectacle in itself.

And when she has stowed her delicacies into two shopping baskets and turns to go, the seller calls out a farewell, *Ciao, bella!*

These two Italian words might be translated as, "Bye, beautiful." But that's not quite right; it sounds a little patronizing. It was meant here as a real compliment, appreciative and at the same time humorous—as if he could still see in her the attractive young woman she had been long ago. And how does the old lady react? With a bittersweet smile she says one word to the gallant stall holder: *Magari.* Which means "If only."

Magari—the whole drama of life in a single word. If only. Because this old Roman woman has no illusions. She's long since learned that you have to say goodbye to many things. She retains her wish for beauty and admiration, while accepting that those things are far behind her. *Magari*—if only.

And I thought about how the climb from the market to my monastery, Sant'Anselmo, is getting increasingly difficult for me. *Yes, that's clever, perhaps even wise: when the years can no longer be hidden, gloss over them.*

With pride and melancholy.

With humor, in all its forms: with poking fun, like Roman Herzog and me; with harmless joking, like Elisabetta and her friend; with wise resignation, like the old Roman lady in the market. Or clothed in a big theatrical gesture like the Roman emperor Augustus who, when he was already mortally ill, summoned the Senate one last time and appeared in makeup and carefully combed hair, saying after his short farewell address: "If you liked my performance, applaud again."

Most of us, in our final years, won't be in a position to expect applause. So, we'll need humor even more. Because aging is actually both extremely funny and extremely sad. We've never been so good: rich in experience, rich in learning, rich in understanding, insight, and knowledge of human nature. And now, precisely when we've never been so good, our strength starts to diminish.

Didn't we always wish for this serenity, this self-confidence, this inner freedom, this sovereignty? Just when we're where we've always wanted to be, our body starts sending increasingly clear signals that it's had enough. A decisive battle is in the making between our body and our ego, with a predictable end.

"Dying is shit." Thus author Sibylle Berg sums up her horror in the face of our mortality. And speaks to us from the heart. It's unbearable to think that one day we'll no longer be here. Once in this world, we never want to leave it. We hope for life in all its glory, fullness, and intensity—in all its charm. And we never stop hoping against all reason to avoid death, that dreadful cleft that runs through creation.

Some people in old age wake up in a cold sweat. Once again the coast has come a bit closer—that foreign coast where our ship will be dashed to pieces. We can see the end of our journey and we're scared stiff. As far back as we can remember, we've cruised the open sea and felt nothing but an endless expanse around us, feeling that it will go on forever—happily taking it for granted.

There would be tomorrow, of course, and then the day after tomorrow, and next year, and the year after that, and we would always encounter incredible new things—things we hoped for, and unexpected things that would keep us on our toes. What was ahead of us was incalculable and infinite. We drew our courage to face life from the inexhaustible richness of what lay ahead.

And then suddenly there's land in sight. First a small, dark strip of coastline on the horizon, it comes closer with every new morning. It dawns on us that the days of our life are numbered. We cannot correct our course. We can look back, but not turn around. All these years we've lived in blissful error, intoxicated by an illusion. In a future we now can foresee, we'll no longer be a part of things; we no longer eagerly await what lies ahead. This realization takes us by surprise.

But can you ever make your peace with mortality, with having to die, with this "shit"? Or is futile rebellion the inevitable result of our pride? I remember an obituary. It was an indictment, a reproach against God written by the husband of the deceased. There was no trace of peace or reconciliation with a merciless fate.

"Where were you, God?" it said. "Where were you when my wife was stricken with an insidious disease and received the wrong treatment for nine months? Where were you when she was torn from life after selflessly nursing her sick mother for many years? Where were you when she passed away two days after her mother? And why are you punishing me with her cruel death?"

The bitterness of this obituary touches our hearts. It confronts us with the awful abyss of our existence. It would be obscene to recommend humor. However, I've often found that the elderly, the sick, and even the dying show nothing of the bitterness with which Sibylle Berg curses our mortality, or the bleak despair with which relatives react to the suffering and death of a loved one. What I remember much more is people facing the ends of their lives serenely and in a manner that can only be called cheerful.

This joy is, as it were, a product of their faith in Jesus Christ. It arises from the confidence of being destined for a new life after death by the grace of God. Their humor is like the little brother of their faith. This attitude, which can probably be termed *serenity*, is best represented by Sister Bertwina, the last German Benedictine nun in a Korean convent. When I visited her there, she was just celebrating her hundredth birthday.

Since I wanted to show her my full respect, I arrived with a bouquet of one hundred tea roses. Sister Bertwina received the roses with shining eyes and clapped enthusiastically when I serenaded her on the flute with improvisations on Korean and German folk songs. That she could still feel joy after all she had been through is a miracle. After the Korean War, in the fifties, she went through the daily torments of a four-and-a-half-year imprisonment in a North Korean prison camp, including the customary torture.

This didn't seem to have had any effect on her state of mind; in any case, she didn't harbor the slightest grudge against her former tormentors.

"They were also just people," she told me. "They had their orders and who knows how much pressure they were under. . . . I already forgave them when I was in the camp." That settled things for her. She was reconciled, and that reconciliation had saved her from bitterness. Also, Sister Bertwina laid no claim to happiness, so disappointments haven't harmed her.

When I asked her if there was anything I could do for her, she answered, "No, my only problem is that I'm feeling so great." She said goodbye with the words, "See you in heaven, if there's still a place free for us." When I got into my car, she waved to me cheerfully with both hands. I'll never forget this. Sister Bertwina with her joyful serenity was at least one step ahead of me. How lucky to have met this woman. A great moment.

I'm learning. On a sultry summer evening three years ago, I wanted to have a quick dip in our monastery's swimming pool, was too hasty, and stubbed my second toe hard on the edge of the pool. It hurt terribly—periosteum injuries are the most painful ones. I gritted my teeth. I didn't have time to go to the doctor. Later I noticed that the toe was crooked. Hitting the edge of the pool must have broken it, and it healed at an angle. Should I go to the doctor and have it broken again and straightened?

What the heck, I told myself. *It's not worth it anymore. For the remaining ten or fifteen years, it's good enough. It's not perfect, but I can walk, and that'll have to do.* You see, at my age you include death in your plans. And I think I showed an appropriate sense of humor.

2.

It's Easier Not to Plan

The alarm clock tears me from sleep at the usual time of ten to six. A new morning dawns over Rome, and I would give everything not to have to get up.

Last night I was up late again. I replied to a pile of letters and twenty emails and wrote a column for the German magazine *Bild der Frau*. It was two in the morning when I switched off the desk lamp. That's not unusual; after midnight when the day's work is done and my head is free, I often get a second wind.

That's when I have my creative phase. When I have these moments of inspiration, I need to seize on them, and not get bogged down in brooding over an upcoming lecture, like a student over a homework assignment. So as long as the ideas flow, I keep at it. Four hours of sleep should be enough.

Four hours of sleep ought to be enough. It always used to be enough. What is it my father used to say in his final years? "I must get up, otherwise my whole mind will go to sleep." And the morning is my time. I have my best ideas. While I'm asleep, so much accumulates that needs jotting down immediately. And today, I have nothing to complain about.

How often do I wake up in the middle of the night because of jet lag after traveling to Rome from Manila or New York? Instead of tossing and turning, I will go back to my desk, say some psalms, and work for another hour. But not tonight; I slept through. So why the overwhelming desire to stay in bed?

Half-awake, I say to myself: *How long can this go on for? How long will it be at all feasible? Until you're eighty? It's just under six years until then. That's not much. You might have more time. Your parents got to eighty-five. Why shouldn't you live to be the same age?*

Eleven years—that's not much either.

It's better to banish such thoughts immediately. Not that they scare me—I've never thought about my end with horror; I don't get depressed like some do at the beginning of each new decade of their lives.

Nevertheless, I do notice changes in myself. I have to admit that since seventy, nature is putting the brakes on me. I'm becoming slower. Four hours of sleep is at least one hour too few. Recently my legs have started bothering me. After giving a two-hour lecture followed by discussion, if I remain on my feet the whole time, sometimes I hardly know how I'm going to get down from the podium, even though it's only a few steps. It's in the genes. My father also complained about his legs when he was old. Although, he did stand from morning to night at an ironing machine in the garment factory.

Come on now, I say to myself. *Your work is waiting. You've got a lot to get through today. The new strategic plan, the meeting of the construction committee—at some point the renovation of Sant'Anselmo has got to be finished. So get out of bed!* "The early bird catches the worm." The classic kick in the pants, delivered to me, by me.

I'm sitting on the edge of the bed now. But I'm still not ready for action. Do I really have to do my morning exercises? Maybe I'll shave first. The face looking at me from the mirror sets me back again—I don't look very enthusiastic. But I get a grip on myself and do some stretching exercises, then take a shower, alternating several times between hot and cold water. And, finally, the Notker I see in the mirror can smile at himself. *Well then.*

On the way to the first Divine Office I meet two Indian students in the elevator. We smile and silently acknowledge each other as we collect ourselves for prayer. Here in Sant'Anselmo we say only the bare minimum, and preferably nothing at all, to one another early in the morning. I enjoy the silence, and that too has changed over the years. As a young monk, silence was hard for me. Now I'm one of the advocates of continuous silence in the early hours, at least until breakfast is over.

When I enter the church I'm completely focused on the Liturgy of the Hours, and the moment I chant the first notes of the Gregorian antiphonal I'm finally wide awake. It's great starting the day with singing, in the choir with my confreres, the text of the Psalms on my lips. I forget myself in the process and look to God who created me and will accompany me through the day. The Psalms always show me new examples of how firmly I am anchored in my faith—nothing could do a better job of encouraging me and giving me energy at the start of the day.

Then the singing comes to an end. Together with the others, I leave the church and go through the cloisters heading for the refectory, our dining hall where we have breakfast together. It's a magnificent Roman morning; the sun has already risen, and its rays are warming up the cool morning air. Blackbirds are singing. I quietly whistle their melody, and one hops closer. She looks up, glances at me, and whirs away—I'm probably not the partner she had in mind.

As I enter the big hall of the refectory, my usual confidence and serenity has long set in. Nothing can shake me today. The working day can begin.

It might sound as if I still have big plans. But I don't live in the future. Nor, however, do I live in the past. I live in the present. I don't have the time—or any desire—to look back at my life and take stock. I've got better things to do than rehash old stories. It may sound crazy, but I still feel, at almost seventy-five, as if life is still ahead of me, endless.

An eighty-nine-year-old confrere from an Austrian monastery once said to me, "I still know why I get up every day." I feel the same way. As long as the spirit of optimism doesn't leave me, the best years are not in the past; and so far every new day instills in me the spirit of optimism—even if getting up in the morning now takes more willpower.

It's not as if I suppress thoughts about my death. I sometimes involuntarily ask myself at night, *Will you wake up again in the morning?* I sometimes think about how many years I've probably got left. (Of course the answer is different each time.)

This is not new. At thirty-seven, driving my little Fiat on the Italian highway from Rome to St. Ottilien after my election as archabbot, I suddenly thought, *What if you were snatched from life by a fatal accident right now?* I remember very well. It was a dazzlingly beautiful summer day; gorse and oleander bloomed in the highway's center strip. *This is splendid!* I thought—and suddenly imagined not living to see the end of the day. It didn't frighten me in any way, oddly enough. *You've had so many wonderful experiences in life so far*, I said to myself, *more than others have in seventy or eighty years*. I would have died then blessed and rich, gratefully satisfied with life. But I arrived safe and sound in St. Ottilien, and my life changed fundamentally.

No, the thought of death has been with me for a long time. In recent years, though, a certain uneasiness has crept in. The driving force of hope is gradually losing its power. The thought of the future no longer consoles and encourages me as it used to. Dying is a possibility at any age, but the certainty of death is a new experience.

Even if my light still burns as brightly as before, I've only got a stump of candle left, and I can't hide that from myself. How long will it last? Another ten, at most fifteen, years? In any case, a meager stock, a pitiful remainder. And a strange feeling creeps over me.

Years ago, dying seemed easier. Perhaps you're more generous with your life when you feel you're drawing on unlimited resources; life feels more precious the less of it that remains.

———•◆•———

Moderation seems quite appropriate where eating and drinking are concerned. For quite some time, I've contented myself with half of what I could eat, and I abstain almost entirely from alcohol. I accept these restrictions willingly because they increase my well-being, just as I enjoy using my new hearing aid, because it saves me from moments of extreme embarrassment. I repeatedly used to find myself dropping off in meetings.

The talk at meetings and conferences is usually in English or Italian, and mumbled, so I have to put twice as much effort into listening. I would be overcome by fatigue, and give meeting participants the uninspiring sight of a sleeping abbot primate. As I said, it was embarrassing, but now that's over. With my hearing aid, I stay wide awake even during the toughest meeting. It's become as natural to me as my glasses.

I'm happy to make this kind of concession to my age, but slowing down doesn't suit me. I want to work; I need to be creative. Some people consider me a workaholic. Maybe they're right. Sitting on the couch and watching TV would be a nightmare for me.

But neither do I have plans or targets—no "government program" or brilliant new idea about how the Benedictine order can be optimized or restructured. I don't even have a concept—for the simple reason that throughout my monastic life, for a wide variety of reasons, I have found I never accomplish my original plan—things always turn out differently from what I want, imagine, or anticipate—and it is a good thing.

I get by better without a plan. I let myself drift—go with the flow in a way I've learned to trust. From my perspective, each task presents itself of its own accord—you could say it finds me.

Then it's up to me to deal with it—to recognize it, grasp it, and meet the challenge it represents. Does something need to be tackled and satisfactorily completed? Well then, let's get started—God doesn't make it easy for us. And when that task is finished, I start the next one. I'm delighted when the new task demands even more commitment, even more ingenuity. And under no circumstances do I rest until I've gotten a good result.

———•—•———

Meetings, conferences, and lectures in the United States, Israel, or India—long-distance flights, time differences, the constant change of climate, and on top of that, air-travel chaos, constant delays, the race to make up for lost time: it's exhausting.

It's rare that a long trip doesn't include cancellations or incidents; sometimes I feel like a juggler in the circus, only without an audience. For a conference of abbots in Chicago, a strike of Lufthansa pilots meant I had to change my booking. All right; I could fly through Washington instead of New York. In Washington, we landed one hour late. The usual irritatingly scrupulous American passport control cost me another two hours. When I reached the gate for the connecting flight to Chicago, boarding had just closed. It was futile to protest; in the States you can't appeal for sympathy like you can in Germany—the ground staff won't soften. So I had to find another flight, and I arrived in Chicago at midnight instead of 4:00 PM. I then had a one-and-a-half-hour car ride. Finally, at two in the morning, there were no more obstacles to a refreshing sleep—at what was, after all, my usual time.

The next day I had appointments from morning to evening. The day after that, I had to go on to Savannah, Georgia, so this time I traveled by car to Minneapolis and took a plane back to Chicago, but that plane landed late, and of course I missed the connecting flight to Savannah.

When was the next flight? "No chance," I was told. "Certainly not today; all the flights are full." Really. It was 11:00 AM. I sat in the lounge of the airport in Chicago, opened my laptop, and started looking for flights myself. I discovered a flight from Charlotte to Savannah. *Well then.*

"Can you at least get me to Charlotte?" I asked the two ladies at the counter. They tapped away impassively at their keyboards, while my feeling of triumph rapidly faded until at last the face of one brightened—good news. In three hours there was a flight to Charlotte, and they put me at the top of the waiting list. *At the top— that has to work. Some passengers always cancel.* And so it was. A small odyssey, and I was in Savannah. Again at midnight.

A day in Savannah, then back to Munich via New York. The following evening, I was due to give a lecture in Münster, and all three hundred tickets were sold. *This time, nothing must intervene.* I arrived punctually at the airport in Savannah, boarded, stowed my carry-on luggage, and cheerfully sat down. And the plane didn't start. We finally took off after an hour-and-a-half delay, and when I looked at my watch as we came in to Newark airport, I saw I had just half an hour to catch the connecting flight. I was never going to make it—it's a huge airport.

Now I had to pull out all the stops. I took out my cell phone, called Lufthansa in Germany, explained my situation, and said, "Please ask the staff at gate B61 to wait for me! I absolutely have to make my flight!" Lo and behold, they really did wait this time. The plane took off into the night sky over the Atlantic, en route to Munich with a contentedly smiling abbot primate on board—who, incidentally, arrived in Münster on time and gave his lecture feeling quite relaxed (but then had trouble stepping down from the podium).

So, yes, it's exhausting, and I rarely take breaks. But staying flexible mentally and physically, searching for new solutions, and taking on the unexpected is still for me what life is about. My previous achievements don't particularly interest me. What lies behind me is checked off like a to-do list; you crumple it up and throw in the wastebasket when everything's been done. In any case, we should beware of being too proud of our achievements—clinging to the past.

———•·•———

My heart is with the future of my order, and this attitude has always invigorated me. Recently someone unexpectedly submitted a proposal concerning our work at Sant'Anselmo, and I confess, at first I was not happy. *Please, not another new idea! For once, can't we just keep to what we agreed on long ago?* After considering it, though, I decided the idea had some merit. Without further ado, I embarked on implementing it, only to find it was some of the much younger confreres who were resisting change. So then, in addition to the work of making the changes, I had the hard work of persuading them.

Sometimes, though, I'm the one who's had enough. *Lord God, does it never end?* I moan. The next moment, God looks at me and says kindly, "Come on, keep going," and I obey. This has, if not exactly a dismaying effect on my schedule, at least a dizzying one—it is chock-full, with an unbroken sequence of lectures, trips, meetings, and quite unusual projects.

I am booked out twelve months in advance, and there are practically no free days. Thank goodness I have the experience of having had such schedules for years: I know that what can be done will be done, and what, despite my best intentions, I find I don't have the strength for will fall by the wayside.

What has always really annoyed me is something else entirely: constantly having to resist the well-intentioned advice to, at last, slow down is downright debilitating!

I know I am no Hercules. In my childhood, I was bedridden for a long time, and I was hopeless at sports—I was the one who ended up in the water when we had to jump over a ditch. Since early on, people have tried to turn me into a hypochondriac: "Slow down." "Don't overdo it." "Think of your health." This was the tune I was offered to dance to, and the refrain was always, "You can't do it; you'll never do it." This is the stupidest form of suggestion I know; rather than help in any way, it undermines your self-confidence, and eventually you do indeed fail.

In old age, the doom-laden chorus is getting louder and louder. After every long trip abroad I have to listen to the same words: "You're expecting too much of yourself." "Don't do this to yourself anymore." "Jet lag is doing you long-term harm." People even prophesy: "You're not going to last much longer—you're overtaxing yourself. If you keep this up, you're going to collapse." "Let go," they say. One of the most popular pieces of advice to the aging? "Treat yourself to a peaceful old age." The word is *retirement*.

I don't know what these admonishers understand about happiness. I don't deny that their concern is authentic, but everything in me resists this uninvited compassion, because it hides a fearful, despondent attitude—a gloomy pessimism that is always convinced that "this can only go wrong, it's bound to end badly."

Oddly enough, it's always the others who get ill. Those who take care of themselves. I, thank God, enjoy fairly stable health—to the surprise of the doubters. What many people probably can't understand is that I draw tremendous strength from my work—from the stresses and even from the misadventures. And steeplechasing is almost my favorite discipline, because after every unpleasant surprise—to my repeated amazement—my mind is suddenly crystal clear and operates calmly as if on automatic pilot, spitting out unexpected solutions. This was so in the past, and it is still the case.

Of course jet lag takes its toll. Of course sometimes pressure in my head prevents me from sleeping. Such small maladies are inevitable. But when faced with a great task, I get to not think about myself—just like a mother whose child cries at night doesn't think of herself. On the other hand, the energy I have to extend to deal with compassionate pessimism is a total waste.

I do find allies. One of them is St. Paul. He writes in his Letter to the Philippians, "forgetting what lies behind and straining forward to what lies ahead" (Phil. 3:13). He was not young when he wrote that. My second ally is the American swimmer Diana Nyad. At the age of sixty-four, she jumped into the sea in Cuba and came ashore in Florida fifty-three hours later after having swum 177 kilometers (110 miles) without stopping and without a shark cage. That impresses me. Because what counts is passion—and then you put up a good fight as long as it's at all possible.

3.

Greetings from Pink Floyd

I still have the words of an eighty-seven-year-old lady in my ears. "As a young person," she said, "you have no idea what it's like to be old." That's probably true. For many years, age remains something abstract. I assume this is, at least is in part, because we don't want to know too much about it. We recoil from this final chapter—it's just not the most attractive period of life, and the thought of it is at least uncomfortable and embarrassing, if not scary. It's enough to know that being old probably won't be much fun.

So you don't lose any sleep over it. And when the time comes, when people on the street look past you or through you as if you were invisible, you tell yourself in desperation, "I've nothing to fear, everyone's as old as he or she feels." This wards off the worst for the moment. Surveys have found old people feel on average ten years younger. Some even twenty or thirty years.

Of course that's nonsense. The body is counting the years, and it's an incorruptible chronicler. It counts methodically, with no intent to conceal true age (in most cases, at least; there are lucky exceptions). The writer Uwe Timm is probably nearer to the truth with his practical definition: "As long as you can still put a sandal on while standing on one leg you're not yet old."

There is some truth in the comforting idea of perceived age, though, because body and soul experience time differently. While the body obediently follows the law of impermanence, more or less punctually presenting the corresponding signs of deterioration, the soul measures itself by a different standard.

It changes; it expands or shrinks, matures or withers, becomes more beautiful and rich or uglier and poor. But it doesn't grow old; it's timeless. It absorbs all we've experienced over time and all the ages we've passed through, and it leads a life of its own beyond space and time through a colorful mix of childhood dreams and the hopes, disappointments, experiences, and insights of later years.

The years don't challenge the soul at all. If all we had was our soul, resolutely vibrant, cheerful, and full of a zest for life, we wouldn't have to speak of age at all. We would speak of fulfillment and repletion. At worst, we would speak of emptiness.

So, aging is not a simple matter. Being old is certainly not as threatening and scary as we're lead to imagine. From a psychological point of view at least, it's the most exciting period of life, as body and soul slowly diverge and the body increasingly gives rise to worries while the soul's appetite for life goes on unabated.

In other words, just as the evening of an ordinary working day is a different experience from the morning and afternoon—relaxation and increasing tiredness for the body, pleasure and fulfillment in the company of old and new friends for the soul—so the so-called evening of life also has its own character.

I propose seeing old age not as the beginning of the end, but as a fully valid third period of life, in which our earthly existence shows itself in a new and by no means repellent way. The duration of old age alone justifies this view. If everything goes well, after retirement we can expect another twenty, perhaps even thirty years—childhood and youth are shorter, so even in terms of quantity, it's no pitiful remainder. And it's in these years that the timeless and ageless part of us really develops.

Think about it: Your struggles are behind you. You've weathered the times of uncertainty. Trials and tribulations are largely a thing of the past. Hormones have more or less settled down. The pressures you suffered under for decades have been released. You are free, free as you've never been before in your life; you finally have time, and you know what to do with it. One person will do a doctorate in the history of art, another will get his hunting license, another will lie on a lounger in the garden smelling a newly opened rose; many want to travel to the foreign countries they've known only from business trips if at all.

The fact that this third phase will certainly end in death isn't relevant. To those in their seventies, at least, surveys have shown that they are enjoying their lives and are more satisfied than any other age group. It seems that everyone else has the wrong idea about age.

In any case, what these old people say about themselves makes total sense to me. I am one of them, even if as a monk and abbot primate, I'm a rather unusual example. I will describe how I'm enjoying the so-called retirement years.

———✦———

This summer I had a two-week holiday in a monastery on Lake Wolfgang. (My annual leave is usually shorter and sometimes canceled altogether.) While I was there, I received an invitation to the Tollwood Festival in Munich, and I must admit I didn't know exactly what it would be like: a kind of Woodstock but lasting for weeks and without the mud? It didn't matter; the offer to perform with my band in the Andechser tent was appealing.

Well, I said to myself, *if Bob Dylan, Mick Jagger, and others from the glorious age of rock music, with their lined faces, still dare to perform, you can do it too—in any case they won't have to get you off any drugs first.* I accepted the invitation.

Someone drove me from Austria to Munich. "Oh yes, you're the father from the mountain," said the security guard at the entrance to the Tollwood grounds with a glance into our car. Apparently, he'd seen the television interview I did on the summit of the Dürrnbachhorn with Werner Schmidbauer. "Tell you what, I'll let you through here, then you won't have so far to walk to the tent."

I already felt at home, even though I'd never been here before. The guard signaled his colleagues, so the way was open all the way to the Andechser tent, and after a short sound check (the other band members had arrived earlier) we were ready for our concert, two hours of rock music in the tent from 7:30 to 9:30. Although, I have to admit I sometimes left the stage. A concert that long is too much for me these days, plus I don't have the time to rehearse enough songs to fill an evening program. I'm lucky if I find two or three hours at Sant'Anselmo a few days before our performance to put on our CD and rehearse my parts on guitar and flute. So I played in two of the four sets, and my band did the rest on their own.

Apart from the singer, our band always has the same members it did in the good old days when I was archabbot of St. Ottilien and the others were students at our school. That's a long time ago now; my fellow musicians have also grown older, but unlike me, they aren't aware of it yet.

And it's still tremendous fun for everyone. For example, we did a performance under the southern sky in front of a large audience at an arena in Pescara, Italy, dubbed "Pink Floyd Sends Greetings from Pompeii," which was unforgettable. As was our show soon afterward in Seeon, a magnificent monastery on a lake island in Bavaria. Seeon has made a name for itself as an event location, and I was invited to give a lecture there to the managers of the Ingolstadt hospital. "Bring your band along," they said. After the talk at dinner in the magnificent, colorful refectory, I still had my doubts about playing in this setting, wondering if rock and Baroque really went together. But a little later the set got going, and I enjoyed playing as usual, and the experience was a real miracle.

That's what the head of trauma called it anyway—it was absolutely unbelievable how all differences disappeared immediately, all formalities forgotten, all inhibitions gone. Everyone danced until they were ready to drop: consultants, lawyers, administrative staff, the whole management team, men and women, all mixed up together. Rock and Baroque do go together after all.

This was followed the next evening with a performance in Carinthia, Austria, inside the venerable walls of St. Paul, where on the following morning I would be saying the celebratory Mass and preaching, before flying back to Rome in the evening.

———•——

Let's catch our breath. I know the whispers that are going around. From one direction I hear the heavy sigh, "He'll never fit in with the rest of us." From another the warning, "Be careful, you're the abbot primate; please behave accordingly." And then there are my primary-school classmates, who to this very day visit me in Rome from time to time and exclaim with amazement, "Werner [my birth name], you haven't changed a bit!" What can I say?

Yes, it's probably true—no one who's known me for a long time will notice any big difference today. I've never been antisocial; my constant activity isn't a gift of old age. And while it's true I'm the abbot primate, the expression "befitting one's social status" has never meant anything to me.

How I go about my work, how I define my role and how I shape it, is my decision, and anything that could possibly qualify as "unseemly" I clarify with the Lord Jesus Christ: he's my model.

Of course I'm going to make mistakes, but I don't lose sleep over it, because I know nobody's perfect, and I don't need to be either. Christ himself appointed the far-from-perfect Peter as the leader of his followers, a person who even disowned him when it came to the crunch. So we can go wrong, but we shouldn't let ourselves be influenced by the worriers. I'm reminded of a grave inscription in the Campo Verano, a cemetery in northern Rome, which says, *Non flectar*, "I will not bend."

"Slow down a bit," some say. "Please tone it down," say others. And I say, "Come with me." Come, for example, to Altenburg Abbey close to Vienna for the interreligious song event. The first benefit concert was held there in 2012 for restoration of the nearby Jewish cemetery that was devastated in 1938. The abbot of Altenburg had urgently asked me to participate. "We need you, and don't forget your flute!" Oh no, another appointment. But miraculously I found a gap in my schedule, and I traveled there without knowing what awaited me.

With four hundred visitors, every seat in the monastery's library was filled. I was in good company. The singer was the chief rabbi of Vienna, a man with a sense of humor and a powerful voice; another rabbi played the keyboard, the Protestant bishop of Vienna was drummer, and a gentleman from the local finance ministry was saxophonist—completing the spectrum, as he had left the Church.

Behind us was the boys choir of Altenburg, and we gave it all we had, playing Yiddish songs and gospel songs, and receiving enthusiastic applause at the end of every number. Afterward, when everyone was standing around in the richly decorated, brightly lit library, still suffused with the music, a high-ranking politician from Lower Austria came up to me and said, "You know, Abbot Primate, our church in Austria is at such a low ebb. If it wasn't for you Benedictines. . . . You're the enlivening element."

The enlivening element? I am grateful to hear that. It's exactly what I want to be. It's exactly what I wish for my order as a whole—to have a stimulating effect on society, in all the places in the world where we're represented: this is one of the three great visions that guides me.

To achieve this goal we must of course be alive ourselves, and this requires abandoning well-worn tracks. I can't determine the pace of the world, I have no influence on the great upheavals of the time, but we mustn't isolate ourselves from these changes and lose contact with the world, with life, with other people. After all, what are we here for? For the world, life, and other people.

I think my continuous connection with the world of rock music has had very positive consequences. First of course for myself, because I love rock music, and after all these years it still epitomizes vitality and zest for life. Second, however, because I reach many people through this music.

For example, in Barcelona, I was to give a lecture to the executives of an international corporation. In the introductory session the moderator told them about our band's performance supporting the legendary Deep Purple. When they didn't quite believe him, he referred to the YouTube entry "Deep Purple mit Abtprimas Notker Wolf—Smoke on the Water." (Yes, we played the song together.)

As if on cue, all the participants took out their smartphones and were too busy tapping and swiping away to listen to my words of welcome, but with this I had won them over. Abbot Primate Notker Wolf supporting Deep Purple? On stage with Ian Gillan and Steve Morse? An introduction like this greatly increases receptiveness. It breaks with convention, makes it easier to talk to people, and spares me the usual small talk.

Sometimes the rock music even merges informally with the Christian message. During our Tollwood performance in the Andechser tent, a banner with the words "Highway to Heaven" hung above the stage, a combination of the AC/DC title "Highway to Hell" and the Led Zeppelin classic "Stairway to Heaven"; I would never have worked it out myself, but of course it fit superbly. And many of the songs we play are original compositions and reflect our origins at the St. Ottilien mission monastery.

My favorite song is "My Best Friend," and if you listen carefully, you'll realize that we're singing about Jesus Christ, the only one who doesn't abandon you if all your other friends let you down. To play it safe, I introduce such songs myself, also so no one in the audience thinks my black Benedictine habit is just a particularly crass stage outfit.

———————

Travels abroad, stage performances, meetings, conferences, lectures, interviews, TV appearances, magazine columns, books, and building projects: admittedly some things in the repertoire traditionally belong neither to the responsibilities of an abbot primate nor to the role of an almost-seventy-five-year-old.

One side effect is the challenge of managing my schedule. This involves never-ending tinkering: appointments constantly have to be changed, inserted, or added. Because of special requests and spontaneous inquiries, half of it ends up being improvisation, so no one else could possibly be expected to get their head around it. That's why I take my schedule into my own hands.

Another side effect is amateur psychologists having reasons to whisper about me. "He needs it," they say. "He can't do without it. He's determined to make a difference and leave his mark on the history of the order. He can't stop for fear of losing his importance." Or, "He's running away from himself."

It's true that I have a duty as abbot primate. It's also true that I see it as my greatest and finest duty to open as many doors to the future as possible for my order. That would scarcely be possible if I didn't keep on the move, respond to contemporary trends, try out new and perhaps even unheard of things, while at the same time giving an example of the vitality I wish for my order. We've both reached a certain age, my order and myself—in the case of the former it's 1,500 years. Wear and tear are not alien to us.

But that shouldn't be a reason for either the order or me to slacken. Of course no one is irreplaceable. *But as long as we live, we're needed.* That is a possible answer to the questions confronting anyone in the third phase of life. We may be unimportant as individuals, but the ideas we promote, the efforts we make out of love or conscientiousness, are not.

We're needed. And it's wonderful to be needed. It may be quite strenuous, as in my case. But when people ask me, "How do you manage it? How can you stand it?" the answer is simple: Joy is my lifeblood—joy in my work, joy of meeting people, joy in music. Also joy in nature—the different shades of green of the oaks, pines, cypresses, and olive trees in the southern sunlight. Joy in the sea I like to sit by and swim in. Joy in the warm golden tone of the evening light flooding into my study.

And especially joy in the Liturgy of the Hours with my confreres, and in the Eucharist, the Lord's Supper, when I unite myself with Christ in order to live from this unity. The memory of his death and resurrection renews my own hope of life each time.

Joy makes you free. So it doesn't bother me that people always need things from me, that I'm assailed and under pressure from all sides. Passionate commitment lets you make any work your own, even when it's imposed or unavoidable. The freedom arises when you tackle work with joy. On the other hand, if you work morosely and halfheartedly, plod listlessly through your quota of tasks, you'll always feel confined and pressured.

So, once I've put my mind to a task, my yes is always 100 percent. I throw myself so completely into the work that it gives me, and others, pleasure, and people say, "He made the project his own; he never wanted it any other way."

I also believe that fundamentally liking people—all people, wherever you encounter them, on the doorstep in Rome or in China—will keep you young. You don't come off like many older people, for whom the pleasure in meeting foreigners is spoiled by xenophobia. The fear that what is different could be dangerous is known to increase in some people with age. They shut themselves away, isolate themselves while on journeys, fear unfamiliar food and hygiene methods, and prefer to keep solely to their familiar and extremely clean surroundings.

That's not my cup of tea. Every day people approach me because I also approach them. It's "Good day, Abbot Primate. I know you from television," as I'm getting off the boat on Lake Wolfgang; or, "Look, there's the traveling monk," when I check in at the airport (even though I'm in civilian clothing); or, "I have an audiobook by you. I like it so much that sometimes I stay sitting in my car at the end of a trip, so caught up in it that I can't turn it off," when I'm in makeup for a TV appearance.

In these moments, politicians would feel flattered. What I feel is like someone coming home to his people, protected and surrounded by the whole human family. I'm indifferent to my prominence—it leaves me cold—but I enjoy being welcome, being at home with people, being at home on this earth.

4.

Famous Old Men

As a novice and young monk at St. Ottilien, I revered and admired the old mission fathers. St. Ottilien was founded in the nineteenth century as a missionary monastery with the task of reviving the former missionary ethos of the Benedictines, which had died out in the Middle Ages. I looked forward excitedly to being put to the test as a missionary myself—as far away from home as possible, preferably in Africa or Korea.

And these old fathers had actually lived the exciting life I was dreaming of; they'd courageously survived for decades among "wild" peoples, put up with unimaginable conditions, and braved the most adverse circumstances to the glory of God. They'd been threatened by snakes and treacherous tropical diseases, had faced death daily, and now, after a life full of danger, had returned to their home monastery— active monuments to Christian heroism, surrounded by an aura of adventurousness in the service of God. I admired them. These old men were my models.

However, their active days were largely over. There were two who spent their days walking up and down the upper library corridor at a snail's pace. One of them, Father Callistus, had been imprisoned in a concentration camp in North Korea and returned in poor health, dragging one foot due to a slight stroke; the other one, Father Sigismund, had been an African missionary and also returned marked by illness, with similar mobility problems.

If the door to the library corridor shut behind them with a click, Father Callistus would ask "Who's that?" and Father Sigismund, the more mobile of the two, would turn around and report. This, as well as their endless discussions, could be heard over a wide radius, because, suffering from deafness, they talked at maximum volume.

Their humor was incidentally quite coarse, which is typical of veterans. When our former archabbot Suso returned from a trip to Africa and, still somewhat shaken, described an attack by a crocodile that had torn the leg off someone who was with him, Father Callistus said drily, "And I always thought crocodiles only ate grass."

After all they'd been through, these old missionaries were but shadows of their former selves, but in the context of their pious self-sacrifice, I found this mixture of coarseness and callousness doubly fascinating. I liked them; I revered them. I felt the opposite of arrogance in their presence—their life's work spoke for itself.

Other confreres of advanced age were also good role models. Even one whose unfortunate, somewhat malicious nature didn't exactly recommend itself as an example. When I was plunged into a crisis during my novitiate and doubted my qualification for the monastic life, it was he who temporarily became my hero. *If someone with such a difficult character has managed to persevere and resist all temptations*, I said to myself, *then you'll succeed as well.* It helped.

The Benedictine monastery has always been what one would call today a multigeneration house. At that time I was one of the youngest, and dealing with old people including the sick and dying, and those with dementia, was part of everyday monastery life. It was instructive, it was stimulating, and the stubborn and confused sometimes stretched our senses of humor to the limit.

The elderly were also respected; the youth cult was not yet upon us, and you could talk about old men without in the same breath calling them ossified and unrealistic as almost automatically happens today, especially with reference to the pope and the Church. In my area, in any case, things looked different, also later on when I was archabbot.

To give just two examples of great old men, we had Father Felix with his unspectacular heroism, who occurs to me as immediately as does Prior Paul, to whom I forever owe a debt of gratitude as a shining example. I would like to talk about both of them.

In 1982, we embarked on the founding of our new monastery at Digos on the Philippine island of Mindanao. I'd been archabbot of St. Ottilien for four years, had so far not even dreamed of founding a new monastery, and actually didn't think this project had a chance because, who of our people would take on this burden? Who would shoulder the privations and the primitive life conditions, at least at the beginning, at the other end of the world?

Wherever was I going to get the founding team? From which monastery should I draw people? I needed experienced missionaries, but I couldn't in good faith promise much more than blood, sweat, and tears, to quote Winston Churchill. What was more, our African monasteries, which had long been suffering from a shortage of staff, mutinied. Shouldn't I rather dismiss the whole thing as unrealistic?

I started to feel hopeful when Abbot Odo in Tokyo gave his consent. Father Edgar from Münsterschwarzach let me persuade him to take part in what could only be called an adventure, to put it mildly. Now I only needed a third person.

"Try your luck with Father Felix," advised our mission procurator, and I thought, "Felix would have to be mad. He's already been in Africa. He won't be keen to start again from scratch at the age of sixty-two"—there was nothing in the Philippines except a vacant plot, tropical heat, and swarms of mosquitoes—but lo and behold, Father Felix was mad.

"God bless you," he said smiling, and agreed to take part. At sixty-two, he ventured anew into the unknown like Abraham.

The initial period was very hard. They had to learn a very different language, adjust to an equally different mentality; meanwhile they lived in Philippine stilt houses, which were not much more than wooden huts full of ants, spiders, and mosquitoes. Could one really expect that of an old missionary?

Father Felix shouldered all the hardships without complaining. He came to St. Ottilien on a few occasions but always went back to his island after a short time, and when I went there myself several years later, I couldn't believe my eyes. On the empty plot of land was a monastery with a church, guesthouse, kitchen, refectory, and library surrounded by palms, cocoa trees, banana plants, and a teakwood plantation.

I held Father Felix in great esteem. He was no genius. No one would probably have seen anything extraordinary in him. He most certainly wasn't a daredevil; sometimes he was small-minded and hesitant. Yet he was loved by everybody—by his confreres because of his straightforwardness and his modesty, and by the local people because he had come so far in spite of his considerable age to help found this monastery. As a confessor, he engendered the utmost confidence and succeeded in bringing priests who had long gone astray back to the priesthood. He will have felt he was just doing his duty.

In 2013, I visited him for the last time; he was ninety-three, bedridden, and close to death. The idea was to take him back to St. Ottilien so he wouldn't be a burden to the confreres in the Philippines. But they were totally against this. They were attached to their *lolo*, their granddad, and weren't prepared to let him go.

It was nice to be with him. We joked around a bit; Felix grinned and was happy. I also thanked him. Now that he's dead, it can certainly be said that his was a thoroughly successful life. What began in vermin-infested wooden huts is today a lively community of thirty monks who farm and produce cheese and milk.

Mangoes and papayas grow in the monastery garden, and about two hundred patients a day receive medical treatment at the small dispensary on the monastery grounds. We even have a study house in the nearby city of Davao, in a breathtakingly beautiful location with a view of the sea and Mount Apo. To finance this new complex, the confreres have created an orchid farm, which is stormed by Japanese buyers.

Probably, none of this would be in existence if Father Felix had chosen to spend his twilight years at St. Ottilien. Nor would there have been a happy Father Felix greatly esteemed by everyone, after thirty-two years of watering geraniums, watching TV, and reading newspapers.

Father Paul was pretty much the opposite of Father Felix. He rarely left St. Ottilien, because he was our prior—before and during my time. When I released the eighty-one-year-old from his office, I wanted to know how he had survived the trials of his life. His answer revealed his old sense of humor. "I preferred to annoy others rather than be annoyed myself," he said. "It keeps you healthy. And second, Reverend Father, don't take anything too seriously in this world, especially not yourself."

When I was a young novice, Prior Paul was a second father to me, and as archabbot I wished all my monks could be like him—so unshakably calm, so unerringly disrespectful, so mercilessly direct, and so loyal.

But Prior Paul was unfortunately, or thank God, unique: a giant of a man, son of a mayor, he observed life from the lofty vantage point of someone who takes nothing and no one too seriously, least of all himself. His ridicule of anyone who took themselves too seriously was notorious— he calmly gave them the runaround and countered them with a concrete wall of subtle irony. Here he was merciless.

Born at the beginning of the last century in the Allgäu, he probably came into the world with his sense of humor. Not, however, with his self-possession, which he taught himself later on. In school, when one of his teachers was putting down his colleagues in front of the students, and constantly venting his anger and making derogatory remarks, Paul was repelled by this exhibited lack of self-control. It provoked him to team up with two friends to put a piggy bank in their dormitory and pay ten cents for every uncontrolled outburst of anger. "After half a year we had ourselves under control," he told me later. "Since then no one's been able to get us worked up."

Prior Paul is the stuff of which good stories are made—many of which are in circulation. Once, an excited novice came to him and ranted wildly about the conditions in the monastery. Such outbursts are not uncommon; now and then young people in the novitiate lose their heads, which usually happens when the abbot is away. Paul was listening in silence to the stream of invective when suddenly the novice grabbed the big Christ's thorn plant on the window ledge and smashed it at the feet of his unmoved prior. The young man came to his senses and stammered, "Father Prior, what should I do now?" All Paul said was, "Pack your suitcase."

Prior Paul shaped my generation. What have I learned from him? That in a leadership position, humor can carry you a long way. That being straightforward and honest can take you even further. And that you can go the furthest if you also are unimpressed by cardinals' crimson robes, by presidential titles, and by company cars.

In this respect, Prior Paul was an exemplary Christian, because it is perfectly in accordance with the teachings of Jesus Christ to expose the vanity of those with authority. Vain people and bluffers had a hard time with him; he provoked them, but in such a way that they could step down from their high horse and experience relief.

Paul died at the blessed age of eighty-seven. In the opinion of the doctors, he should have already suffered a heart attack at the age of sixty, because this big, heavy man, who was a keen reader of crime novels, was equally keen on the cigars and liqueurs that accompanied his leisure reading. When he was already very old, he sometimes lost his balance in his room, and then we had conversations like the following:

"Oh dear, yesterday I fell again; I was lying there on my back."

"What did you do then?" I asked. Given his weight, this was a cause for concern.

"Well," he said, "I rocked back and forth like a beetle until I landed on my stomach, then I crawled to the bedside table and finally managed to grab the phone and call the confrere who takes care of us."

Humor and serenity in the face of precarious health, right to the end—Prior Paul's life was an unforgettable example for many, just as was the quiet heroism of Father Felix in the Philippines. Imagine if my predecessor had relieved Prior Paul of his duties for St. Ottilien at sixty-three and sent him into retirement.

His light would have continued to shine, but under a bushel basket, and others would not have seen it. And to continue the metaphor, I would have gone along on my way a lot less enlightened.

So, I advocate for not demonizing the contributions of older people. We impoverish ourselves if, blinded by an obsession with youth and misled by foolish stereotypes of "ossified" and "unrealistic" old people, we let only young overachievers lead. They lack the inner richness of many old people. Also, character traits such as unpremeditated kindness, which makes dealing with people so gratifying, usually only appear at an advanced age.

In my opinion, Cardinal Augustin Mayer embodied this characteristic like no other. I'd already made his acquaintance in the sixties, because my studies at Sant'Anselmo coincided with his term as prior and rector. Later he became secretary of the Congregation for Religious and Secular Institutes in the Vatican and was consecrated bishop and appointed archbishop and, finally, cardinal and leader of the Vatican Congregation for Divine Worship and the Discipline of the Sacraments.

The positively touching affection for Sant'Anselmo, which he retained throughout his life (how often I heard him refer to it as *il nostro caro collegio*), went back to World War II. He together with Paul, the subsequent prior, formed the monastery's protective troop, as it were. (I need to note here that Augustin Mayer looked totally unsuitable for military tasks: he had a delicate constitution, and somewhat resembled a male Miss Marple, but without anything like her cunning and courage.) He died at the age of ninety-eight, and until then I visited him once a year, always on the second day of Christmas, which is usually reserved for visiting elderly relatives.

One afternoon, half a year before he passed away, I was in the cloister. Sant'Anselmo was bathed in glorious summer sunlight, and I was explaining the large building complex to a group of visitors from Münsterschwarzach when the heavy wooden door from the freely accessible forecourt opened. The fragile but still quick-witted Cardinal Augustin Mayer approached, pushed in his wheelchair at a leisurely pace by two sisters. Surprised and delighted, I hurried to meet him and extended a warm welcome. "Good day, Your Eminence, what brings you to us?"

"Well," he said simply, "the sisters here come from America and have never seen Sant'Anselmo before. That won't do. So I thought to myself, you must show them Sant'Anselmo."

Such kindness! He found it unacceptable that the two American sisters had never seen his beloved Sant'Anselmo with their own eyes and, despite his nearly one-hundred-year-old body, had assumed the role of tour guide himself. I lifted him out of the wheelchair and set him on a bench in our cloister, and there we sat for quite a while chatting animatedly in the sunshine, like Philemon and Baucis in front of their hut.

5.

The End Is Nigh

I think Italians don't see growing old as such a tragedy. It's probably because, as a society where the family and family life still play such a strong part, they find it easier to see life as a cycle of birth and death. For them, the aging and dying of one generation is just as natural as the birth of the next generation.

Just go out on a summer evening in my district, Testaccio. Every trattoria has tables and chairs out on the street, and from half past eight on, all the seats are filled. All through the Roman summer, people enjoy eating out in the open air.

It's amazing how family-oriented it is. Six or eight people turn up, with the youngest still in a pram and the bowed old aunt supporting herself on her niece's arm. Even the retired professor from next door didn't have to be asked twice.

They start the evening by greeting acquaintances at other tables; the amazing progress of the offspring in the pram over the last seven days is commented on; and then they all order and eat and talk the whole time as if they haven't seen each other for ages.

I'm not wearing rose-colored glasses; it is a pleasure to watch Romans dining. It's amazingly civilized—out of respect for the old people at the table—but it's informal, cheerful, and often very noisy too. To observers from the north it feels like a play. And they're quite right, but it's not a drama or a tragedy; it's a comedy enjoyed by both old and young.

This social environment could also be the reason the elderly on the streets of Rome radiate a confidence you don't find so often in Germany. I remember two small, fragile ladies of advanced age—clearly way over eighty—who had sought shelter in the same house entrance as me during a summer downpour.

We nodded to one another and exchanged encouraging words while waiting, but the rain never let up. One of the ladies asked whether I could read the name on the street sign—her eyes were probably no longer very good—and after I answered she took out her cell phone.

Five minutes later a big, dark jeep appeared in the little side road with her son or son-in-law at the wheel. The two old ladies climbed up into the ostentatious vehicle, and once sitting comfortably in the dry gave me a small triumphant smile through the rainy side window as they roared off. "See, young man, that's how you do it nowadays," I read in their satisfied expressions.

With all the similar experiences I've had here in Rome over the last twenty-five years (which is how long I've been living here), it's hard to disagree that aging is easier in Italy. You fight aging more fiercely when you feel like you've missed out in life, perhaps missed something crucial—that you haven't bucked authority enough, or that you never hit the jackpot. Older folks here don't feel like they've missed out on something.

So at least here in Rome, those feelings play a lesser role. People radiate a contentment I find exhilarating when I take my occasional Sunday walks on the Aventine. I meet so many young couples holding hands or standing silently in a loving embrace under the orange trees in the park, or looking down raptly from the viewing platform at the city, at the green curves of the Tiber bordered by the tightly packed houses of Trastevere, with the dome of St. Peter's Basilica rising up prominently behind them.

Don't you think you might forget your wrinkles if you took part in natural, sociable multigenerational rituals like the evening meal in a trattoria and a Sunday afternoon stroll under the orange trees?

Although at Sant'Anselmo I'm largely isolated from everyday life in Rome, my life is defined by similar experiences. There is the security I get from life in the huge extended family of my confreres and sisters; and there are still the reliably recurring customs and rituals of each day—but don't confuse ritual with routine.

⸻

Our everyday lives, because of their routine nature, are not very elevated. Rituals add highlights to the day. For a short while they lift us out of the everyday and remind us that we were made for things higher and more beautiful than a mundane existence with no room for thought or imagination. Rituals are small celebrations—this applies to our collective Divine Office for which I interrupt my work four times a day, and equally as much to those nighttime family meals in a Roman trattoria. They enable us to repeatedly stop and reflect so we don't get bogged down in everyday duties.

For me, the Divine Office above all is an incomparable source of strength, as it permeates the church with the simple tone sequences of Gregorian chant, which embody the earnestness and unshakeable faith of a past era. I would never want to forgo the praise and thanksgiving before and after meals either—a ritual, in the form of saying grace, that was common among families until just a few decades ago. Even in North Korea, a mayor once specifically asked me to say grace before a shared meal.

Whether the purpose is culinary pleasure, keeping the family together, or holding a dialogue with our God and Creator, customs and rituals provide a strong framework within which you can move safely and with relatively little effort. They simply make your life easier, because you don't have to reinvent your daily schedule and way of life every morning.

Rituals save us from two extremes to which we are susceptible: stuffing our day with hectic activities, and letting the day pass unused, then sinking into lethargy. And rituals can provide stability that is urgently needed in one particular life situation: when you retire after thirty, forty, or even fifty years of working life.

———◆◆———

Your desk drawers are empty, the office door shuts behind you for the last time, and you drive away from the company parking lot—you said goodbye to your colleagues and boss earlier with champagne and a cold buffet—and the next day you wake up a pensioner.

At first it's like a holiday. But the longer this goes on . . .

It's not that the world fades. It's you that fades. Increasingly, you feel marginalized. Pushed out of the flow, you wash up on the shore, like driftwood on a riverbank. You stop being of use, you make way for others, and unwillingly, you gradually become a spectator of life. The number of people for whom you're no longer important increases steadily. You offer your opinion, but it no longer carries much weight with others; they politely take note of what you've said, but because it originates from a bygone era, they no longer think it worth considering and regard it as a mere curiosity.

With feelings ranging from disillusionment to dismay, you find the outside world increasingly empty, and your own potential in decline. Sooner or later you are surprised to realize you no longer have a part to play, which leaves you at a loss. You're reminded of the Peggy Lee song, "Is That All There Is?" You have the CD on the shelf but don't like listening to it.

What name can you give to this experience—this plunge into insignificance, descent into unimportance? Dethronement, perhaps? Abdication? It's particularly hard if the life you are withdrawing from is very busy. Then retirement can hit you like an emergency stop, going from a hundred to zero. You were used to excitement—strong stimuli and intense experiences—and now you don't know how to feed your soul. It's hard too if the descent is from a high position. After fifteen years on the management board, you are at a loss without a secretary, driver, and company car— without influence and privileges, you feel like a drug addict in withdrawal.

The stream of invitations slows down to a trickle and finally dries up completely—you are simply forgotten. One of the most moving sections in Sven Kuntze's thought-provoking book on getting old, *Altern wie ein Gentleman* (Aging like a gentleman), describes how quickly this can happen. Just after he retires, Kuntze attends a meeting of the Federal Press Conference. He was a highly regarded correspondent covering the capital for public broadcaster ARD; now he is an onlooker, and no surprise, he is ignored by most of his former reporter colleagues. Chancellor Angela Merkel deigns to nod in his direction when she spots him at the back. He no longer plays a role. The game is over. The end is nigh.

Going forward from this point, are you nobody?

Yes—in the world where you practiced your profession for decades, you can expect the world's ingratitude. And no—in a new world that now opens up before you. At your advanced age, you have to retrain and start practicing for this third stage of life.

The first thing you find out is that when you forfeit your professional role, your only choice is to become—a person. Stripped of all external attributes of usefulness, facing life as just yourself may involve tapping into qualities that you might not have needed before; for some, this is a new and challenging experience.

Taking this a bit further, you could say age shows what a person is really worth, reduced as it were to mere human existence.

Maybe you've dreamed for years about being free of the shackles of working life, of finally just being you—and now you find yourself saying, *I'm stressed out, and I'm stressing out the people around me. This is hard work. Because, who am I really?*

As you can see, retirement can mean facing a lot of changes. At the beginning of the third stage of life, we are faced with a mountain of tasks. When we start our career, other people equip us and support us, but when we stop, we have to deal with the situation more or less on our own, and society hasn't prepared us for it.

Over time, the qualities we start to discover more of a need for include willpower, strength of mind, patience with ourselves, independence from material things, equanimity when dealing with setbacks and disappointments, and don't forget humor and self-confidence, which now need to be based more and more on true self, and not on our once-fantastic looks.

We need courage—courage that over time comes to look like the silent, unobtrusive heroism expressed in Mae West's famous saying: "Growing old is not for cowards."

If you have a partner to support you through the inevitable change, you are lucky. He or she can tell you again and again: "You're not your job title—the trappings, the status, achievement, and roles. Remember you the person." But as nice as family support is, as important as a storm-proof partnership is (as my Italian experiences show), this is just the beginning of the real work.

For the moment, however, it is enough; this is quite a lot to cope with. Let's take a breather and pick up the thread again in the next chapter.

6.

The Train Hasn't Left

Well, you've entered your new phase of life with body and mind more or less intact. Friends and family have cushioned the fall from the professional world, and your everyday life has begun to be governed by a new rhythm—after a few stumbling steps, you've made the transition from the tarantella to a slow waltz.

Now you're confronted by fundamental issues: Should you find a new way to rev things up or accept slowing down? Should you put in regular hours at a health club in the hope of prolonging your life a bit or act as if nothing's changed? Is it enough to know you have a nice apartment in a warm spot like Majorca or Tenerife to spend the winters in, or will deciding how you shape the next twenty or thirty years require more imagination than that? And what can you do to prevent feeling superfluous? To ward off the specter of boredom and purposelessness? Who or what might be able to keep you alert and active until the end?

Well, one thing at a time, and there's no rush—which is now what it's all about. The first thing on the list is creating a framework for your new life—to give your everyday life a certain regularity with pleasant habits that can turn into favorite rituals. Thanks to your newly acquired freedom, there's a wide range of options.

Here are a few concrete ideas:

- Meet regularly with your three best friends on fixed days once or twice a month.

- Sing in a choir with weekly rehearsals and two concerts a year—which would have the additional advantage of increasing your circle of acquaintances and even friends.

- Shop at the farmer's market on Saturday morning and then visit the café there—like every regular habit, this will get around; your acquaintances who also shop at the market will know when you're there, and that café will become the meeting place for you all.

- Go to church every Sunday, sing lustily, pray out loud, and celebrate the Eucharist.

- Start up a salon. Every two or three months invite all the people you know plus someone with something to say that he or she knows more about than the others there. After the discussion, everyone chats over cheese and wine—you will make a wealth of knowledge and skills available to your circle of friends.

The list could go on forever. These activities don't restrict your newfound freedom, and they will fill it with life; plus, you'll have taken a big step into the new era.

It's not enough to give your life a framework, though. It won't help against the nagging doubts that plague each of us in old age: *What am I still needed for? What still gives me a right to exist?* It won't replace the picture that belongs in the frame. What about your passions and ambitions—does growing old mean burying them?

There's a great danger that you have gloomy pictures in your head as you enter the third phase of life. These tenacious clichés come from outdated ideas of old age and retirement, which no longer have any foundation in reality. But they can still cause damage, paralyzing us with their poison and putting us in a kind of old-age trance. Don't throw in the towel! You can even still do something entirely new: *I wrote my first book at sixty-five.*

No, death doesn't cast its shadow as quickly as all that, and until that happens, human beings need something to do. What's true of the first two phases of life is also true of the final one. Life must have a certain level of difficulty if it's to be satisfactory. This should be self-evident, but it is often forgotten under the influence of the reigning philosophy that we should make things easy for ourselves. Dangerously, our innate tendency toward inertia is encouraged by the flood of images of blissfully smiling people taking things easy. Let me be blunt: this philosophy will make you feeble.

So let's start something new. With our knowledge and our skills, we have what we need for this new phase of life—and there's such a wide variety of activities on offer nowadays. We can be consultants, speakers, and helpers in developing countries, where we may be useful in education, in hospitals, and perhaps as observers of elections. We can get involved in political parties, in associations and clubs; we can be "grandparent readers" for children from migrant families in elementary schools, and we can act as tutors.

We can volunteer in countless fields—lead tours in museums, for example—or look after newly arrived refugees who at first will depend on help for absolutely every aspect of life. Adult education centers and universities are open to us too, so why not learn one or two new languages?

One of my acquaintances began his studies in old age and completed his doctorate on the artist Joseph Beuys—he finally had the time and no other demands and was able to fulfill this last lifelong wish. What would his last years have been like if he'd subscribed to the common attitude and said, *It's not worth it anymore; that train left long ago?* For ten years, he would have done nothing while watching other people his age accomplishing things.

It's a perverse turn of mind that leads people to persuade themselves they're old and weak. They let themselves become dominated by negativity and a focus on futility. Trains leave the station, and trains arrive too—there's always one for us to catch. Even if the journey is going to be over soon, if we get on a train, we get to see a part of this beautiful world we didn't know. One last time, we delight in experiencing something new.

We don't have to study art history; our ambitions can be more modest. I think of my father, whom I always picture in his later years sitting at the kitchen table mending pants, often until midnight. He was a tailor. When I finally got him away from the ironing machine at the factory, he started taking jobs in the neighborhood. He seemed to really enjoy mending; he sang and whistled as he worked. When he died, he was satisfied with life and could leave it serenely.

So don't give up. Set yourself goals. Get passionately involved in new areas of activity.

But beware worshiping the idol of efficiency. This whip-wielding slave driver has chased us around enough already in life. From now on, nothing's urgent anymore; nothing we do has to be measured by whether it's "worth it"; and success will come or not, without anxiety. If we let this new life be dominated by old standards of purpose and benefit, we'll face stress and disappointment, because nothing will come as quickly and as easily as in the past. We're free; we may even regain some of the pleasures of childhood—we can rediscover the joy of play, and we're allowed to dream again.

———◆———

Unlike in childhood, our dreams are not mere fantasy now, because we have ways and means of making dreams come true. Instead of dreams I would rather speak of visions. Realistic visions. In my opinion, visions are indispensable at any age, because they inspire, they make every goal appear achievable, and they release energy. I have always been guided by visions, not plans; and today I enjoy having three big visions. I've already touched on them at several earlier points: now it's time to go into detail.

During my time in Sant'Anselmo these three visions have come to resemble something of a program. The first, as I've already explained in some detail, is the vision of a vibrant Benedictine order that affects and stimulates the world outside the monastery walls with its spiritual vitality.

The second vision is of a thorough and enormously costly renovation of this large building complex called Sant'Anselmo, which has been thought through architecturally down to every last detail.

Seen from Trastevere, our monastery on the slope of Aventine Hill in the south of Rome rises in the distance with the air of a well-established and seemingly unshakable fortress of the Christian faith. Seen at close quarters, it's clearly showing signs of age and was already in this state when I was appointed. Some parts that date from Sant'Anselmo's founding at the end of the nineteenth century are crumbling, and other parts no longer fulfill present-day needs. I've spent a lot of my time in Rome—actively supported by a confrere from Switzerland—raising money for the renovation, planning it, and supervising the implementation. Maybe I'll succeed in completing this before I leave Rome.

My third vision is the modernization of our university, the heart of Sant'Anselmo. Students from our monasteries all over the world are inducted into the Rule of Benedict here. Unfortunately, our way of teaching has become a bit outdated; we've become stolid while the world around us changes faster and faster. It's no longer sufficient to analyze the text of the Rule of Benedict from an academic point of view, and to lecture in the traditional manner on philosophy, theology, and liturgy.

The Rule of Benedict is undoubtedly important—it's the basis of our identity—but every inch of it has now been researched. What we've neglected is contact with the modern world, and the future of our university is therefore at risk. With our one-sided historical orientation, we can no longer compete with other Roman universities.

I want to turn our university into a platform for dialogue, based on our tradition, with the spiritual trends of the present. Interreligious dialogue is inevitable nowadays. As the culture our monasteries exist in is becoming more pluralistic, we can no longer assume those around us share a Christian point of view. How do we react? How do we relate to other religions?

Do we seal our windows tight or throw them open? Do we condemn pluralism as a work of the devil or seek a dialogue with all those who influence the spiritual climate of our time? These are existential questions we should not be afraid to ask ourselves. And who knows—perhaps the answers will have consequences for life inside our monasteries in the long term.

Does all of this have to be done before I resign? At most the progress of our construction projects is in my hands. For the revival of our order, I can only provide motivation. As for modernizing the university, that's a very tricky issue. A building submits without a word to everything you plan. But a university is a living organism that can be hurt by drastic changes. And there are cherished habits, and the all-too-human tendency to be lazy, so sometimes I have to assume the role of troublemaker, or dynamic mover and shaker. That's something I like doing, trusting in the uplifting effect of new ideas. The fulfillment of my dreams would be to say goodbye to a restored Sant'Anselmo that is imbued with a fresh, modern spirit.

Until my last day in Rome, I'll do my utmost to achieve my three visions. Not least for my own sake. Because however much it's true that joy is my lifeblood, it's also true that I owe my inner resilience to these major tasks.

7.

A Privilege of Old Age

As long as you're still young, the future holds the promise that all your wishes will be fulfilled—it has possibilities in abundance, and it will allow you to share in that abundance. Later you learn that disappointments flow from the same source, and that it's by no means inexhaustible. And eventually, in one person the foolhardy hopes will be replaced by bitterness; in another, by humility; and in a third, by faith. (By faith, I mean putting your trust in God as readily as you used to put your trust in the future.)

Rome would certainly not be the right place for me if I were based in bitterness. Even a foundation of humility would be out of the question given the major tasks I'm confronted with. All that remains is faith, trust in God's help, and that's why, for example, I go down to our cloister every evening where there's a mosaic of St. Joseph in the wall.

I stand there, say a short prayer, and ask for the success of the construction work, because my advocate for our renovation project is St. Joseph. When I check my mail later, I discover that another few thousand euros have been granted for Sant'Anselmo. No, not always, but sometimes. Some readers will be shaking their heads. Are prayers in front of an image made of mosaic tiles appropriate in our enlightened times? Probably not. Wouldn't the grant have been made anyway, without my evening visit to St. Joseph? Possibly. But would I have applied for the money without being aware of my heavenly backing? Would I have tackled the reconstruction project with uncertain financing? Would I have started an adventure that has been going on now for ten years?

When we began, the costs of renovating the roof alone exceeded our entire annual budget, so the situation was actually hopeless. And today? We have a private office in the United States that employs professional fundraisers, and I have the reassuring certainty that I'll leave no debts to my successor when I retire. It's true that many people have contributed to this success. I myself gave lectures for many years, and on my travels throughout Europe and the United States asked for donations, but without St. Joseph . . .

Let me tell you another story.

I was visiting a big Benedictine monastery in the United States. The abbot took me around the whole building, showed me all the rooms, and, lo and behold, everywhere there were pictures and statues of St Joseph.

"You may laugh," he said in explanation when I asked him about this, "but I took over this monastery with massive debts, and I'll pass it on to my successor with a surplus of several million. That I owe to St. Joseph." This was an immensely capable man—capability is the first requirement in such a role, of course. But boldness is second and luck third—and luck is as unpredictable as boldness in old age is rare.

Something else comes into play; I would call it pious realism. Time's always running out—every major undertaking is pointless on the basis of the facts—but faith lets us retain that foolhardy confidence of youth as we get older. We don't need to worry that time's cornucopia is almost empty.

Anyway, success is not in our hands; it's given by God, as he's always given it. We only have to set out with confidence in his blessing and do our part as far as we can and while we still have the strength for it. It's with this conviction that I turn to my advocate in heaven every evening. And I must say that I've been heard.

I readily admit that my faith seems naïve. The abbot of the American abbey prefaced his explanation by saying, "You may laugh," but laughter was far from me. I know faith in God is a source of strength that doesn't run dry even when you can't rely on bodily power as much as before, and you'd rather be unreasonable than reasonably give up hope. For me, the unreasonable goes very well with the reasonable. What would be the point of measuring faith with reason? If faith is only valued in terms of what's reasonable and explicable, it becomes as dry as a fir twig that has lost all its needles. What would be the good of it?

No, I prefer to base my thinking and acting on my life experience. It teaches me that many things happen between heaven and earth that can't be explained by reason, and don't necessarily need to be. So, I run our construction project as professionally as I can, and at the same time I trust in the promise of Jesus: "Ask and it will be given to you . . . knock and the door will be opened to you" (Matt. 7:7 NABRE).

St. Benedict, incidentally, took a similar view and in his Rule advised the abbot to be piously unconcerned about material matters: "He should not be worried about monastery assets that are possibly inadequate; he should rather remember what is written in the Holy Scriptures: 'But seek first the kingdom and his righteousness, and all these things will be given you besides' (Matt. 6:33 NABRE)." Faith involves a certain spirit of adventure; you have to be willing to be surprised by God. And as you get older, you recognize there are possibilities worth taking into account that don't fit neatly within cautious reasonable planning.

You see experience overriding reason in old people. They can hold contradictory concepts at the same time, which seems odd to some people, while others suspect a break with reality. But while outsiders wonder whether these old people can separate the reasonable from the fanciful, wisdom from folly, couldn't it also be a sign of the wisdom of age?

Repeatedly throughout your life, you've weighed your own experience against existing knowledge, contemporary ways of thinking, and prevailing opinion, and then you've drawn your own conclusion. In this way you've gradually brought your own interpretation to bear on things and circumstances. By old age, you've probably come to lightly disregard much of what the rest of the world considers to be incontrovertibly true and self-evident.

I, in any case, understand wisdom as being able to judge freely and independently and having sovereign power over my thoughts. A lot of experience has to be absorbed into your own thinking before you reach this state, which is why wisdom can certainly be attributed to age.

———◆———

Sechzig Jahre und kein bisschen weise, sang Curd Jürgens. "Sixty years old and not the least bit wise." This very popular song is frequently appropriated by people who loudly claim that in spite of their advanced age they aren't wise either; rather, they're proud of not having learned anything.

Well, this might appeal to someone who relies on the youthful charm of the incorrigible daredevil, but I don't think much of it. I prefer people who've learned with age. Plenty of people repeatedly make the same mistakes. I find those who've become wise while not seeming old much more interesting than people who seem old without having become wise.

So, for example, I like the mischievous wisdom of a Bhagavān, who provoked everyone with his insane humor—he was original, but also extremely clever, and a freethinker into the bargain. I also suspect that in the case of Curd Jürgens there is a good amount of coquetry involved, because you can hardly avoid being wiser at sixty than at twenty. Wisdom doesn't quite come automatically—some people do become more foolish with age—but most people become wiser. In any case, wisdom in my opinion is one of the highly gratifying privileges of age.

And there are many others. When I was planning this book I came across numerous benefits of age and even came to the conclusion that the advantages significantly outweigh the disadvantages. This surprised me a little, because I hadn't thought about it before. I drew up lists of what we gain and what we lose with age and found in the end that the list of benefits is longer than the list of losses.

On the plus side are strengths such as patience, humor, serenity, knowledge of human nature, inner freedom, sovereignty, and of course wisdom—at least a dozen strengths in all. And on the minus side, I count only three things: loneliness, poverty in old age, and physical decline. (Bear in mind, I'm not saying everyone will reap all the above-mentioned benefits.) Could this be true? Am I being too optimistic? And what about the privileges of youth, the loss of which would also have to show up on the minus side after a certain age, such as light-heartedness, optimism about the future, liveliness, and vigor?

I then considered that life circumstances can get worse. Many old people suffer from loneliness, the loss of friends and familiar people to talk to, toward the end of their lives. Infirmity and frailty can assume terrible forms, so that death is a longed-for release. Poverty in old age, mentioned before, can really wear you down—it's a hard fate for those it affects.

But these disadvantages are not age-specific. Impoverishment, sickness, and loneliness can occur in any phase of life—even death can come much earlier. But the benefits of old age are a gift of our later years and thus true privileges of old age.

And as far as the privileges of youth are concerned, well, that time has passed for us, and it isn't necessary to dwell on it here. A lot has always been said about the privileges of youth, and everybody has experienced them firsthand, whereas the privileges of age come only with time. Also, the strengths and benefits of age are missing from the public conversation, as if they aren't worth talking about.

Thank God, age doesn't oblige me to be timid. So I have decided: no false modesty. There's plenty to celebrate and a lot to laugh about. I think age is good for the character (with some exceptions), and that traits like wisdom and serenity significantly improve our quality of life in later years. In short, we must remember that we can still expect enrichment in old age.

———

What does the wisdom of old age consist of? Basically, the ability to distinguish a mountain from a molehill. This is a great art, and the beginning of all wisdom. Having observed how throughout our lives our opinions and principles have repeatedly shifted, we recognize the extent to which they are influenced by trivialities—such as when something you swore was absolutely essential is suddenly unimportant. With age, everything gradually acquires a more stable value.

To an extent, you know now what matters, what has to be taken seriously, and what deserves to be ridiculed. You are no longer confused by trivial matters; in this time of life, you can concentrate on the essentials.

This inevitably leads to skepticism about the utopian exuberance of youth, the hysterical tone of the media, and all the excitement in the spirit of this age. I'm always grateful for my pipe, which I can puff on perfectly unmoved while the world goes wild over a triviality.

You know the games that are played everywhere, including in the Church; you're not fooled, and you enjoy seeing things in a very different light, assessing them from a different perspective than the chorus of opinion leaders. I delight in the treasure trove of insights and experiences I've amassed, which I am now in a position to draw on.

You certainly need a solid foundation of practical, usable knowledge if you want a reasonably accurate picture of the world, but this doesn't make you wise. There is a specific kind of knowledge, though, which is part of the wisdom of old age—namely, knowledge about the past: history. Nothing is more foolish than the modern disdain for the past, because without knowledge about the past, each generation would be clueless, having to reinvent the wheel.

It is only we old people who know that the same or a similar thing has happened before—a different form, perhaps, but the same substance— no reason to get excited. How hectic the world would be if we left everything to young people! When younger people believe they've found the philosopher's stone, we can always put things in context. We can calm a situation down considerably by reminding everyone that most phenomena in this world are fads and thus transient.

When young we tend to take everything seriously and see many things as tragedies because we are experiencing them for the first time— hence the extreme emotions of young people. We elderly people, on the other hand, have seen things come and go over time; we've learned to see things as emerging and changing, continuously developing, in a state of flux, with each phase of rather short duration. From this perspective, we can call ourselves historians. While all young people see is a jumble of fragments, we ensure with our stories that the web of existence doesn't fall apart, that the major connections and likely directions of things are recognized. There's no harm in being a little proud of this role we have thanks to our age. No; no more panicked reactions. Anyone who gets worked up about the same situation again and again hasn't learned anything. We make our peace with what, after all, can't be changed.

When it comes to human nature, we can be at peace there too, with the quirks and particularly annoying habits of our fellow human beings, a further gift of the wisdom of old age. We learn first of all to accept people as they are, and basically they're not very different from one another. Although we all attach a lot of importance to our individuality, it's usually not very marked. In reality most of us snap at the same bait and thrash from the same hook. Remembering this saves us from the error of taking personally what is only human, and from calling something a character flaw that is quite simply part of our nature.

We've achieved a lot if we get this far. For the simple reason that it puts a stop to one of the most bothersome human characteristics: the tendency to blame people for the same thing again and again, and heap reproach on them. Beware though! If you really want to understand people, you have to go further. You must love them completely and unconditionally.

Only by looking at other people with love can you see all their potential—how they can be if their individual possibilities and skills are fully realized. This is the only way you can do them justice—and incidentally yourself as well. When you see people with love, you don't see through them—that's cheap—you see their hidden but real nature, and you appreciate them for it. Profound understanding is impossible without love.

This is just one example—a particularly clear one—that wisdom isn't the accumulation of knowledge but, rather, a certain attitude toward life. I am using restraint and offering an example rather than arguing my case because this secret knowledge about the fragility of the world and all happiness needs to be handled with discretion. And anyway, wise people don't show off what they know; they intervene, but guardedly, and bearing in mind that all simple formulas—all common explanations—fail given the complexity of life.

Must everything we think or do stand the test of logic? By no means. Not everything we gather in our trawling net over time will fit together. But we will probably have a use for all we've collected someday. As we sift through our catch, we often can't say how and when—life is unpredictable. This is why the experience of age keeps us from presuming the worth or worthlessness of anything. Living with contradictions and inconsistencies is ultimately more honest and wise. I, in any case, will continue my visits to St. Joseph.

And finally, perhaps it takes some wisdom to realize that our youth was not as carefree and cheerful as it appears in the rosy light of memory. To have life ahead of us is not pure pleasure, and to have the greater part of life behind you is not pure horror. Anyway, I know no one my age who seriously wants to be twenty again.

8.

We Are Envied

When I was archabbot at St. Ottilien, I would invite guests from outside our community to join me at my table in the refectory. I once happened to overhear a guest sitting two or three places from me remark to our prior, Claudius, "Your archabbot seems to let nothing upset him." Claudius replied, "That's precisely our problem." And it's true. I simply can't get worked up about anything.

At the beginning of the 1990s, I had a traffic accident in which the car was totaled. A car swung out on a bend on the highway and forced me to make a sudden evasive maneuver. I jerked the steering wheel, lost control, and my car spun on its axis, crashed into the guardrail, and was thrown back again. Thankfully, the truck behind me had braked in time and stopped the traffic. In those days, I smoked Antico Toscano cigars, and when the police arrived I had already lit up and was calmly smoking. Shock, vexation, anger? I've always preferred to leave such emotions to others. There was one time, however, when I was almost driven up the wall.

I had flown to South Korea for the election of an abbot. It was a routine matter, but at the beginning of the meeting a young monk stood and asked, caustically, "What are you Europeans actually doing here?"

It was aimed at me, and of course it violated our Benedictine practices, but it was also a serious offense against the Korean code of behavior. I hesitated.

At that moment my gaze fell on Father Herbert, who was also there and had taught me a lesson fifteen years earlier when some people in Sant'Anselmo had succeeded in winding me up and I had lost my temper. That evening, Father Herbert took me to task. I've never forgotten his words: "Notker, what happened to you today? We have so much respect for you because you never get ruffled, and today you lost control. You really disappointed me." In South Korea, I remembered this incident, and the tense moment passed.

I then replied to the irascible young monk: "I'm not here at my own request. I'm only doing my duty, and as soon I've done it, I'll get on the plane and go back to Germany." This defused the situation. Afterward the older confreres came to me and apologized for the impropriety of their younger colleague. Would they have also done so if I had rebuked him sharply?

Really, I have no talent for getting worked up. I feel ridiculous. I'm simply not made for it.

In the Philippines once, a confrere drove me from the airport to the monastery in a pickup loaded with pieces of iron on a road slippery after prolonged rainfall. My driver proceeded at considerable speed, which didn't worry me, but sometimes he skidded, and when he had to brake suddenly, we turned, slid into the ditch on the opposite side of the road, and there was a tree in front of my window. I looked at him. "My dear confrere, that wasn't necessary," I said. "I don't need a tree; it's not that urgent."

It was the same in Thailand with a half-blind missionary at the wheel, who took up the full width of a three-lane highway; the same in the interior of Africa, where I had a rough landing in a banana plantation after a hair-raising ride from Dar es Salaam. I rarely get upset at things like this.

It's strange, but I always ask myself immediately, *What would be the point of getting excited? How would that help? Not at all.* And I regain my composure—now and then with the help of a couple of whiskies. This helps me in situations like these.

Some kind of solution, incidentally, always materializes without any help on my part. Take Father Felix from the Philippines, for example. On another trip, he was taking me to the airport when the pickup got a flat tire. When we went to quickly change the wheel, we found the truck had no tools, no car jack, nothing we needed. But whether Father Felix was trying to come up with an answer to my question as to whether this was his way of trying my patience, along came the brother of one of our monks on his motorized tricycle, who got us out of trouble.

—————

As you can imagine, the life of an archabbot or abbot primate is ideal training in serenity. And Prior Paul is a role model here too, of course. Also, early on before my time as archabbot, I studied Zen intensively. This is what I took away from the experience: Just be here, be present. Don't let your wishes and thoughts stray; don't picture what might happen and what might go wrong; concentrate on this moment.

So, when people ask me what my plans are, I say, "I don't know. I'm happy to get through the tasks that fall to me each day." This doesn't mean things always run smoothly. And I'm not claiming to be perfect either; everything is an experiment, and I learn from the mistakes. If something doesn't work one way, I try another, and I don't shed any tears over solutions that prove impractical.

I'm not sure this approach is generally advisable; not everyone's professional life is suitable for working like this. I'm extremely fortunate to be my own boss. Everyone is eventually their own boss with retirement—then they can relax. It's goodbye to perfectionism, goodbye to pressure to perform, goodbye to self-reproach.

Goodbye to self-reproach? Well, maybe not in every case. You may not need to prove yourself anymore, and that sure is attractive, but over your life much has accumulated that can weigh on you—broken friendships, quarrels within the family, all kinds of mistakes—so you can still find reasons to reproach yourself.

Some people are plagued with the feeling that they've done practically everything wrong in their lives: that they have failed to bring their children up properly, failed in their profession and in their marriage. This is just when there's a danger of falling into depression—when the hustle and bustle is over, the stress has ended, and you have time to think.

Once depression sets in, no amount of reasoning has an effect, the energy loss is so rapid. It's as if the soul is suddenly engulfed by an ice age. Through the lens of such hopelessness, a person sees his or her life as a complete failure. It's much better if we can realize early that this new period of life is a realm of freedom—we no longer have to think in terms of success and failure. Finally, we can banish from our mental inventory measurements of performance, whether self-imposed or from outside. From this point forward, our own perspectives, our own motives, are all that count, and we can view our lives in a different, probably milder light: *You know what? That decision in the family or professional sphere, maybe it wasn't so bad after all.* Those tormenting memories can lose their sting—maybe we can relax about settling scores with people.

I know the pressure to perform is a hard thing to shake off. It's ingrained after forty years in the working world. But in retirement, it's not just superfluous; it threatens our psychological stability: because measured against our old standards, we will always feel we aren't doing and haven't done enough, and that we're responsible for things that go wrong when we might have done something. Nonsense! We had our reasons, good or bad, the others had theirs, and now it's done—no second-guessing. We need to change our glasses! We only have to get used to being free.

It can help to talk to really old people about their experiences. You'll discover that for many the best time of life begins with retirement. Always under stress, now they can breathe easily. And with advancing age come freedoms unknown in their youth.

For example, an eighty-five-year-old lady described this to me with great enthusiasm: "Many allowances are made to elderly people, and we can act accordingly. I can talk to anyone on the street, I can smile at everybody, and I can compliment people. No one is surprised. I can talk to anyone without explanation or justification, and when I need help, somebody always responds. In short, everyday dealings with people are easy, so I feel a much greater bond with people in general now than I used to. This makes me very happy."

I must add here that this old lady is an Astrid Lindgren type, who would play on a swing in the park, and she said that in this respect she did feel restricted. "It's not just younger people but older ones too who look askance when I behave too impetuously for their liking. Apparently I'm expected to behave like an old person. Sometimes, for example, I run from my house to the stop to catch the bus. I can still do this for a short distance, although of course I'm out of breath afterward—but this gets me shocked looks: old people don't run! But then, the bus driver always waits for me."

So maybe there are a few freedoms still to fight for, but in my experience, the predominant feeling in old age is one of freedom (as long as there are no severe health problems, of course). Constraints vanish. No more justifying ourselves—perhaps because of our harmlessness.

No more pressure of deadlines—our time is our own. No more social anxiety—people indulge us. And no more guilt—we're not expected to offer or achieve anything, so we're not falling short.

Looking back on your life, you might ask, *Why did I waste my energy on all that? Was it so important to make a good impression? Why did I take everything at work so deadly seriously?* At some point you say to yourself, *This problem is being presented as if it were the most important thing in the world. If it's still here in a week, I'll tackle it—or maybe not.* Then, at last, you know you've reached the stage of serenity.

———•———

Serenity—the next big privilege of age. We elderly are envied for it! Younger people don't want the old to have a monopoly on this desirable and attractive attribute. A surrogate serenity has been in circulation, called *coolness*; it's already replaced the original in the public's perception. But coolness is an act; young people are pretending to be old and cynical. This only proves how great the longing is for serenity.

Life today is at such a fast pace that something is needed to counter the omnipresent chaos, and because you can't fake the wisdom of old age, the next best thing for the young is this counterfeit serenity.

I probably don't need to say that you shouldn't confuse serenity with dispassion—though they are wonderfully compatible. I have found from my appearances on TV that commitment is much more credible if presented in a serene manner; whereas a presentation that is hasty, reactive, and excited undermines all credibility.

Serenity also keeps you healthy. Nervous complaints are foreign to me in spite of my stressful way of life—my state of mind is unaffected by waiting times at the airports, traffic jams, and raging confreres.

Might an aging society become a more serene society, as more people yearn for discretion, restraint, and less excitement? Perhaps this possibility will be borne away on a raging tide of progress—and that would really be a calamity. For my taste, the clocks could tick more slowly—and above all not so loudly.

9.

Dismay

I said before that misconceptions about age are common. But are they all wrong? What about the physical changes we fear? They can't be denied; they're obvious. They're the distinctive mark of age, and very rarely welcome.

So, I'll approach this delicate topic by a roundabout route. I quote two unbiased people, two writers: the recently deceased German Wolfgang Herrndorf, and French novelist Marcel Proust. Both have dealt with old people's appearance bluntly (begging the reader's pardon in advance). The fact is, I can't compete with their insight or directness.

"Pensioners!" thinks the fourteen-year-old runaway Maik in Herrndorf's popular novel *Tschick*, watching from a distance as beige people—dressed in beige and gray-haired—get off a tour bus. Although the group, moving with irritating slowness, annoys Maik, he can't take his eyes off them. The beige pensioners trigger an indefinable repugnance; at the sight of them, he starts to feel dismay and to think about how ordinary people like himself are reduced to such wrecked zombies.

"They're finished," he thinks, "but they don't know it. They're partying the rest of their days away, freeloading their way through the final years of their lives and will hopefully soon throw in the towel."

Herrndorf's description is so closely observed and the teen's language so accurate that it makes uneasy reading. The beige of the senior citizens triggers in Maik associations with rot. Even if, as a mature reader, you try to distance yourself from his observations, you have to admit that such reactions aren't alien, even to us.

A group of elderly people is usually lacking in what Italians call *brio*, the fire, impulsiveness, temperament, and lively spirit of younger people. As described here, this shortcoming can feel oppressive to an observer. *Do I look as cheerless and lackluster as that?* you wonder involuntarily, and with some consternation.

Herrndorf then makes up for what he's done to us in the pensioner scene; the further course of his novel breaks down the overall impression into individual portraits, highlighting what is fascinating about old people: their unpredictability, mystery, wisdom, generosity, and quirkiness.

Herrndorf more than does them justice; every encounter the insecure and struggling Maik has with adults and old people leads him to have greater confidence. But I want to come back to the disturbing appearance of older people and tell a story of my own.

I had arranged to meet two childhood friends in a trattoria. Our last meeting had not been such a long time ago. I entered and looked for them, but the restaurant was empty apart from two old men.

Well, I thought, *I'll just sit down and they won't be long coming.* As I was about to take a seat at one of the free tables, I looked again at the two old men. It was them. My childhood friends. They were already beckoning to me. I hadn't recognized them. I had seen old men with gray hair, and feeling that joyless lackluster aura of old people that had so disturbed young Maik, I had instinctively concluded, *That can't be them; they're too old.*

This bizarre mistaking of my friends for unknown old men gave me no peace. They didn't correspond to the picture I had of them. We'd seen each other recently, and at second glance, I recognized them easily. I think it was the gray and listless impression, which didn't match my memory of their lively personalities.

Do we have two pictures of a person in our mind: one with an ageless freshness that reflects the soul, and one that updates to his or her external appearance and current state of physical decline? Why hadn't I managed to combine these images? Is it that the indestructible is what counts most for me about my friends; the destructible is secondary? Or had I felt a slight aversion to these tired-looking old men and wanted nothing to do with them?

I was probably looking for my friends with my mind's eye. Still, it's disturbing how much the two images diverge when people get older.

For me it was certainly a moment of revelation, but one everyone knows who has met a friend for the first time after fifteen or twenty years. The spontaneous reaction to the changed face and figure ranges from irritation to shock; you involuntarily look past the rounded face, plump body, and bald head and search for halfway-unchanged features—perhaps the nose and mouth.

But once you get into conversation, the irritation passes; your friend is again consistent with the timeless picture you have of his or her character and nature.

Or maybe not.

———————

The most shocking commentary on age is in the seventh and final volume of Marcel Proust's monumental novel, *In Search of Lost Time*. We find something very similar to Maik's reaction to the pensioners, but on a larger scale: for sixty pages, Proust describes the details of physical decline with merciless insight and the same dumb horror of Herrndorf's young hero.

After many years away from society, the narrator attends a matinee at the Paris salon of his old acquaintances the Guermantes. All the society people he used to regularly associate with are there. He goes in and faces what looks like a terrifying masked ball. It seems to him they're all in disguise—everywhere he sees gray wigs, white beards, and masks with coarse, hardened features. They ponderously lower themselves into chairs, ponderously get up again—as if they are wearing lead shoes.

He thinks of a stage performance with actors transformed into doddering old men and bulky matrons, unrecognizable in their grotesque disguises. He's tempted to applaud and congratulate each one. Gradually he identifies all those present, but how they've changed! These masks and beards can't be removed; these faces and figures have been shaped not by theatrical skill but by an accumulation of years.

With one person, lively blue eyes have been replaced with a rigid, piercing gaze; in another, mouth and eyes have disappeared into red bulges; the stuggish bulk of a third person gives no hint she was once a celebrated dancer. "I could have sat opposite these people at a dinner a hundred times," he thinks, "without realizing I used to know them."

His struggle to recognize people shows on his face, and he's embarrassed, but he can't help it. "Who am I greeting now?" he asks himself and thinks of three people who might match what he sees, but it turns out to be none of them.

He gets a name but can't comprehend that it can relate to two completely different people—the graceful lady of yore and the frail old one before him. Have they all become caricatures of themselves?

He discovers many who've improved with age. One looks more imposing with his mane of white hair; in another self-assured gravity has replaced shyness. But with these observations, the narrator is changing his perspective to an extent to his inner eye. And now he gets a second surprise.

"Monsieur d'Argentcourt," he writes, "had become so different from himself that I thought I was standing before another person." This formerly repellent and hostile man was now benevolent and confiding. He is not the only one who seems to have adopted a new personality. The narrator meets a number of men and women who were formerly, as he puts it, unbearable, but who appear to have shed their faults entirely, as if their character has relaxed its cramped stance and their previous arrogance, bitterness, or spitefulness has fallen away.

The whole society suddenly appears in a different, brighter light. I'm glad to find my own experience confirmed in a great work of international literature: growing old does our character good—at least in most cases. There is one weakness, however, that we never seem to discard: vanity.

In the narrator's salon, all these old people have in their own opinion remained young. Everyone sees the signs of age only in others. Though for the sake of politeness they assure the other he or she has held up well, they only seriously believe it of themselves.

Of course the narrator believes he's the only young one among all these old people. Even though they have exactly the same difficulty recognizing him, and some old acquaintances act as if they've never seen him before, everything in him resists admitting that "I belong to them. I'm one of these people." That is asking too much.

The lesson is, roughly, this: These contemporaries, these old people, are not sexy, but they're surprisingly pleasant. Maybe after twenty years without contact, when we meet an acquaintance again, we find ourselves standing before a completely different person, who's changed so much physically and also psychologically that we have to completely revise our picture of him or her. Unbearable people can become bearable and even lovable. And maybe we can be amused to note the changes in ourselves.

In this Parisian salon, in any case, we witness a gracious self-deception. All those present delude themselves to the best of their ability. They don't believe in the gift of eternal youth, but age has crept up on them imperceptibly, and they've accepted each minor change of the body. No, there's nothing tragic about their situation—but time has been cruel to the others.

Isn't the same true of us? Isn't it both extremely sad and extremely funny? You still feel pretty comfortable in your own skin, perhaps better than ever, but the skin fades, the body loses its shape. (I'm not talking about disease here; I'm confining myself to visual appearance.)

⚊⚊

The clearest indication of our physical decline may not be the mirror; it may be the fact that no one looks at us on the street (and if they do, they look away again). We're not interesting anymore. No more of the inquisitive exchanges of looks young people engage in; we realize wistfully that we're always on the lookout for something pleasing, and that what's pleasing is the bodies and faces of young people, in a way those of the elderly are not. We hold no allure anymore.

There's a second part of this: As our physical appeal decreases, we ourselves attach less importance to the external state of our body. Our mood doesn't depend on it. At some point, we realize we can leave off the anti-aging cream and that a crooked toe is not a disaster. We subconsciously formulate the text of a declaration of independence granting our soul considerable rights of freedom from the body. (Of course as a monk I was never involved in the competition, but I can be allowed to some extent to have a say.)

From now on the main thing is health—mobility and the reasonable functioning of limbs and organs—and over time we acquire a strangely optimistic attitude toward life. What we can't do anymore, because the body doesn't allow it, gives us a pang of regret, perhaps, but what we still can do makes us happy.

In this respect, perhaps in the pages of Proust's novel we encounter not vanity but the wise complacency of people more concerned with the equilibrium and serenity of their soul than with their appearance. I think everybody would agree that this pleasant state of mind justifies small self-deceptions.

However, Proust lived about a hundred years ago. Can we apply his observations to our time at all, or is this all outdated? This is the age of the body cult, after all, when even people bursting with health find it hard to accept small signs of age. How then can we come to terms with the discovery that the body never keeps its promise of happiness?

10.

Forever Young

Eternal youth—of course this dream is not an invention of our time. Youth as the golden sunrise of life, age as its gloomy end—we find such images already in antiquity, and they certainly go back much further. Back to the beginning of humankind, probably. Did Cicero and Seneca, who praise old age, find agreement from their Roman contemporaries? Probably not. In ancient times, the disadvantages of the last phase of life were compounded by fewer ways to mediate the unsightliness of old people: toothless mouths, trembling limbs, bowed bodies—definitely not a pretty sight. Who wants to look like that?

Since time immemorial, people have done everything they can to conceal the signs of age. Those who could afford it in Emperor Nero's Rome, including the men, spent hours every day at the hairdresser, "where every hair is discussed, every change in the hairline compensated for and bald patches are hidden by combing the hair forward," mocks Seneca, who finds the efforts ridiculous.

Men and women color their gray hair and paint their wrinkled faces—in ancient Rome and Paris salons. Outwitting age and looking even a touch younger, healthier, and fresher than one actually is—this wish will never go away. As mentioned before, it led even Emperor

Augustus to have himself made up and his hair styled like a bride for her wedding before appearing for the last time before the Senate. We even make up the deceased to look as if they could at any moment rise from their coffins!

A theater of illusions. Everyone sees through it; everyone participates. People let their imaginations run away with them. Isn't there an undiscovered mushroom growing somewhere in the jungle that will stop the aging process? Isn't a formula for eternal youth being developed in a laboratory somewhere? And what about a fountain of youth—a magic bath where you immerse yourself and rise from it young again?

Lucas Cranach the Elder painted the fountain of youth in the sixteenth century, and his painting says a lot about the deeper reason for our desire for youth: Men don't seem to need the rejuvenating bath. In his painting, in any case, it's reserved for women. Only old women are brought here, in handcarts and carriages, and carried on the backs of their husbands, and after being undressed at the pool's edge, they immerse themselves naked in the waist-high magic water, splash around, pour the water over themselves, and rise on the other side of the picture as attractive young women.

Not for a second does the painter leave us in any doubt about the purpose of the exercise. What awaits the women? An exuberant male society drinking and dancing with the rejuvenated ladies before enticing them into the red tent. The fountain of youth, as you see, is a male fantasy. Am I doing women an injustice to suspect they would gladly accept such an offer?

—————

Eternal youth and the recovery of lost youth—they are old dreams. People have always dreamed them even while knowing they would never come true, and in the meantime, they have used any proven means of disguising age.

What's new today is how seriously people take these dreams. What's new is the insatiable hunger for youth, the endless desire for the pleasures of youth (which are by no means to be despised). The frightening idea that the body is no longer acceptable when it loses its youthful freshness. The fact that people start hating their own body as soon as the first signs of age appear, and begin the ongoing repair work in the desperate hope of escaping aging. What's new is the obsession with youth and the fact that the body has become the focus of all promises of happiness.

The body, of all things! The part of us that right from the beginning is, as it were, stamped with an expiration date. The part that's guaranteed to leave us in the lurch—that will only become a source of humiliation for us if we put all our money on this one card. So of course a certain amount of self-deception has always been involved; it helps give us the courage to face the disturbing changeability of the body.

But how minor are the innocent acts of the illustrious guests at the Paris salon of the Guermantes compared with the gigantic self-deception of a whole society that promises itself happiness from anti-aging preparations and surgical interventions? That no longer even thinks it ages, but believes it's as young as cosmetic surgeons and the pharmaceutical industry allow? Have we lost all hope of anything else?

I'm glad that, as a monk, I'm not involved in the competition, as I said. I don't have to think about face-lifts and liposuction. I'm old enough to remember how the obsession with youth began: it was the sixties, with messages like those in two books of Simone de Beauvoir that dealt with her horror of growing old.

Growing old was a disaster, she said, an unmerited insult inflicted on us by nature. Focusing her attention, as if hypnotized, on her own body, all she could see was an unstoppable loss of vigor and vitality and continuous deterioration, so that old age for her was nothing but a pointless final stage, a sadistic joke. An old person was aesthetically a disgrace.

A damning judgment. But it's not totally incomprehensible. You can imagine how humiliating it was for her to be unable to compete with the younger women her life partner Jean-Paul Sartre preferred. She confronts age with the furious rebellion of a person used to success and fame, whom the fates have unjustly denied immortality.

There is a lot of disappointment, bitterness, and hurt feelings. But it's all packaged as the ultimate wisdom of a great French intellectual. And for its time it was the last word on growing old, branding it as an accursed phase of life.

Simone de Beauvoir's profound pessimism coincided in the sixties with an ebullient optimism: to the guitar sounds of Jimi Hendrix and the roaring vocals of Janis Joplin, a narcissistic young generation greedy for life dominated European and American culture. The elderly became obsolete, youth took power, and, let's be honest, was there ever a more beautiful, exuberant decade?

Ecstasy, free love, Woodstock—and I too sat in my student room in Munich and listened to records by the Rolling Stones and Led Zeppelin, electrified, intoxicated, and inspired. Forever young. The rebellious students even had an arrogant but not unwitty motto: "Don't trust anyone over thirty." Parents and teachers were no longer respected authorities, and even in our monasteries the abbots felt a cold wind blowing. They were used to the blind obedience of the monks and were now suddenly unable to count on it.

I'm still glad today that I experienced that time. It gave me a sense of relief. As a young monk I'd experienced personally what it means to have to obey iron rules that have long since lost their meaning. Questions were taboo. Each of us was oppressed by the gloomy feeling that every detail of our life was regulated. These rigid, ossified forms had to be swept away, but the elderly couldn't be expected to do it. It had to be done by young people at the height of their powers—exuberant enough to risk anything, inspired by the splendid delusion that they could make the world dance.

But even such times come to an end. Even rock stars grow old and die. What remains is the music—and the echo of an overwhelmingly beautiful feeling that still manifests in the wish for eternal youth. Since then, it has not actually been dying that's shit—to quote Sibylle Berg again—it's growing old. The unbearable thought of how much you'll miss when your body, at some point, loses its youthfulness.

You do miss quite a lot. Everything has its time, and the most beautiful hopes can become the cruelest illusions if one clings to them long enough. Thank goodness the richness of life is inexhaustible, and when we ask ourselves about the meaning of life, the first answer that comes to mind is rarely the right one.

How many times have we had to ask ourselves about the meaning of everything and find new answers? In puberty, we struggled with ourselves before we could leave behind our childish beliefs and wishes and get a feel for the new horizon presented by adult life. Then life changed profoundly and in quick succession with work, marriage, and children, with more big decisions. A midlife crisis resurfaced questions we thought had been answered.

When we enter the third phase of life, many things we've always accepted are called into question again. With the appearance of the distant coast, we're forced to give answers that will most probably have to stand up to severe tests. Not that there's any hurry, but when the hopes of youth have faded, we'll have to set out once again on a new search. Recently I experienced such a departure with a man I consider a good acquaintance, almost a friend. I'll finish by telling his story.

An Italian professor in his late fifties visited me at Sant'Anselmo. A psychiatrist had referred him to me hoping I could do something to help him get rid of his depression and nightmares. I was able luckily to arrange things so I had three days free for him. We talked for many hours, and I heard roughly the following story.

He was the typical intellectual agnostic you often meet in Italy; in other words, he'd alienated himself from the Church and any kind of religious faith. Perhaps he'd never had much to do with either in the first place, but in any case he felt neither a loss, as do many whose faith has left them, nor any vague hopes of Christianity (or any other religion). He didn't believe in anything and didn't miss anything, or if he did, he wasn't aware of it.

In his everyday life he divided himself between two women, his wife and a young mistress, tried to do justice to them both and—being a consistent person—even celebrated Christmas Eve twice. But for some time now he couldn't stand the tension of this double life. He'd indulged in the young person's luxury of belief in unexploited potential, and he had for a long time clung to the illusion that for him the incompatible could become compatible—now this lifelong lie was robbing him of his inner peace. His lawful family had also been affected; meanwhile his adult daughter was suffering from anorexia, blamed him for it, and heaped him with reproaches. In a word, this man was forced to admit that some things had gone terribly wrong, and he didn't know how to go on.

Soon after our conversation he flew to Moscow to attend a medical conference. He used the flight to listen to a CD I'd given him of an audiobook of the Gospel of Matthew, and it was new for him. For the first time he listened consciously to the Sermon on the Mount, and it was if he was hearing it from Jesus's mouth.

The Gospel so affected and fascinated him that he was inspired to write a text of his own and produced a comprehensive work that he called "The Gospel of an unbeliever for unbelievers." It was a first step. Apparently a door he had never noticed before was now open, and this new path was bringing him closer to answers to his questions. For some time now it has been leading him regularly to the Aventine.

His destination is Sant'Alessio, a Romanesque church not two hundred meters from Sant'Anselmo, where a meal is served to the poor every Wednesday; every week he helps distribute the food, and afterward he attends to the sick in his capacity as a doctor. Recently he wrote to me about his plans to fly to Israel and make a tour of the places where Jesus was active.

"Whoever loves God, understands God," I wrote back—a sentence from the First Letter of John. He will have known what I wanted to say: God reveals himself through love, and with loving eyes you see God— no great theological knowledge is necessary for this. "Perhaps you'll become a believer after all, because you're willing to act like Jesus," I added.

In his case the failed attempt to stay "young" with the help of a mistress had been replaced with a project to become a *new* person.

———

Forever young? Yes, you can achieve this, because there is indeed a fountain of youth—it's just that it's not for the body; it's for the heart and mind. The good news is that human beings can change, even in old age.

The example of my Italian acquaintance proves that faith, like love, is a great and powerful transformer and enchanter, and as long we don't stop searching, as many new ways will open up to those profiting from the common sense of old age as to those in the flush of youth. I would even say that by old age you've tried out so many things—in the case of the doctor, this includes a ménage à trois—most of which has been disappointing in the long run, that you're more open to new experiences.

And apart from that, of course, our final years involve renunciation. In the end, our body works against us. But look at the example of music: through blues, jazz, soul, and rock and roll, we retain a lot of the splendid, wild, high-spirited early period of our life. Should we mourn what's past, and desperately wish back what's been lost? As far as I'm concerned, every appearance with my band is still a miniature Woodstock.

11.

Be Strong and Courageous of Heart

S ome years ago on a train, I got into a conversation with a woman who wasted no time taking me into her confidence. She might have been in her sixties, and there was nothing unusual about her, but she nevertheless captured my interest. She was different. Many people with whom you have a chance conversation sooner or later start complaining, talking about something annoying or outrageous, leading to an "Aren't I right?" to try to get you to agree with them. I never go along with it. But even though this woman talked about a string of failures, she radiated a quiet confidence.

She had just separated from her life partner, who had treated her with contempt for years. It had taken a lot of effort, and there was bad blood, but now she was amazed to find that "I get on better without him. Since then I've been able to enjoy life." At work a younger colleague had recently gotten the position she was hoping for. She had been very disappointed at first but, she confessed with a smile, "above all it was my pride that was hurt and you can cope with that."

What made her suffer most, though, was realizing later in life that she'd made so many mistakes with her children. For example, she'd interfered in the life of her oldest for so long that he refused to talk to her on the telephone and hung up as soon as he heard her voice. "But this reprimanding was just what I found awful about my own mother," she said.

This is why she was on the train. She was on her way to see him "just to give him a hug," she said. "I want him to know how much I love him. I don't want to put it off, because at my age you no longer have all the time in the world."

My traveling companion got off the train before I could tell her how much I admired her attitude. There were things in which she'd failed, but every time, in the process she had discovered a new strength in herself—the strength to cope on her own, the strength to overcome her pride and love her children without making conditions. In other words, she'd gradually acquired a distance from herself; she had unbent herself, and this relaxation had made it unexpectedly easy to do what was difficult.

What did we use to call it when people gradually let go of their exaggerated aspirations? When they stopped compulsively blaming themselves and others? When they developed a feeling for the incomprehensibility of fate, which makes all reproach of others and self irrelevant? When they learned to see the bigger picture without deluding themselves that they understood everything? In short, when they arrived at a realistic assessment of themselves and the workings of the world. Wasn't it called maturity?

Maturity; it's a wonderful gift of age. It puts an end to our struggles; it heals our rift with ourselves and with the world. It saves us from being like an old couple an acquaintance described to me—she was in her early eighties, he in his mid-nineties, and both were still hale and hearty enough to live on their own at home. These two were unbearable, he said. The issue was not just that they only thought of and talked about themselves; it was more that they never failed to find fault. Wherever they went, first they noticed anything that was wrong; nobody could do right by them; there was no restaurant in the world where the service or the food was to their liking.

Everything provoked their displeasure; they literally had the evil eye, and this made them intolerable for everyone. But not for each other. They tolerated each other extremely well. The addiction to criticism, the destructive pleasure in grumbling, forged a link between them, bound them together against a universe of imaginary impertinences. Throughout their lives these two had mutually prevented each other from becoming mature. Such people don't even realize how intolerable they are. (And I can well imagine how intolerable these two were in person.)

Marcel Proust was inspired to talk about unbending instead of about maturity. I like this expression. This describes a person whose mind has lost its rigidity, and who can now breathe more easily and feel liberated. It is as if, little by little, the individual has shed an inner suit of armor donned many years ago to go ironclad into battle. Now it had become superfluous. In old age, there's nothing more to be gained by cut-and-thrust anyway, and this self-possession of maturity makes you better equipped than ever for life.

Because it's no longer success that matters. Now what matters is genuine happiness in life, and that requires freedom of movement— freedom simultaneously to step back from yourself and to reach out to your fellow human beings. Perhaps even to hug them, which is what the woman on the train was on the way to her oldest son to do. Those who remain in their armor are too stiff to be able to embrace others.

The disgruntled old couple provide us with a depressing picture of this rigidity: as immature people they had never been able to shed their armor, so they were frozen in a reflexively defensive attitude, still brandishing their rusty weapons of spite. A pitiful sight. Ultimately people are no different from ripe and unripe fruit. The ripe fruit is a pleasure, and the unripe fruit is hard and sour—in other words unenjoyable.

Why have we as a society lost sight of maturity as a goal in life?

One provocative answer is that everything today has the aim of putting us in a state of eternal childhood. The great dream of the modern age is this artificial paradise. We think we should be allowed to remain children. The first goal in life, to which everything else is subordinate, is thus to have all our needs met. And the second goal is to be young.

Satiation is easy to understand. Small children whose needs have all been met don't cry, don't whine, are easy to be with, and don't disturb anyone. Could this be the deeper reason prosperity is our society's goal? Prosperity promises ease. People who are busy with their digestion—and I mean through any kind of consumption—don't ask questions, either of others or of themselves. An easy, agreeable state of exhaustion prevents them from going into anything in any depth.

"A fat belly, a lean brain," said the ancient Romans; in present-day terms what this means is that everything else remains undigested: all life's experiences, its irritations, problems, and injuries. While the belly works intensively, the mind dozes and eventually shrivels away. It doesn't grow or mature; it remains at the childhood stage of begging, demanding, and wanting.

And what about staying young? Children are distinguished by their lack of concern for the limits of reality. They think everything's possible; dreams, wishes, and reality all blend into one. Many people in modern society are the same. They're so convinced of their uniqueness that no limit that has always applied to humankind up to now applies to them.

They want control of everything; they invalidate even the laws of nature and banish fate from their lives. The consequence is a tremendous overestimation of their abilities and possibilities. Like children they believe in their limitless unexploited potential and are convinced that everything will be better if they're allowed to do as they want. *Vulnerability? Mortality? Not a bit of it! We can change that. A fate that isn't in our own hands? Only a fool believes that old story.*

The wish is stronger than the reality. That's why people today want to enjoy life on earth in the permanent flush of youth. That's why they do everything to live their lives independently of their Creator and the laws of nature. That's why they remain a prisoner of their infantile wishes even when very old. It's as if Western society had entered the phase of the terrible twos, as a growing number of people live under the delusion of unlimited youth and redefine what it means to be human as follows:

The number of years we've lived is irrelevant. Only our way of dressing, speaking, and behaving indicates how old we are, nothing else. Lifestyle is everything. Maturity is not only unneeded; actually, it would be showing our age and in effect giving up: we'd be demonstrating to everyone that we've failed to stay young.

Who would want to be mature under these circumstances?

⸺◈⸺

The main things are to be satiated and to be young. But you *do* get old; that hasn't changed. What has changed is that people aren't prepared when those illusions are revealed for what they are, one after another. So, those who do well at remaining young are likely to do badly at aging.

So we face a choice about growing old. Do we want the hard way or the easy way? Do we want to expose ourselves to ridicule and pretend to be young for as long as possible? Or do we want to come to terms with life in its entire confusing, frightening, and exhilarating fullness, at the price of being perceived as members of the older generation?

I will suggest what might be a reasonable, realistic attitude toward life, if that's what we're looking for here. It can be summed up in two short sentences:

Don't rebel against your fate.

Don't compare yourself compulsively with others.

You can't take either of these to heart too soon, because they'll make your whole life easier. They'll help you cope with disappointments, adversities, and blows of fate.

If you rebel against the merciless passing of time, everything that's not to your liking will bore into your soul as painfully as a foreign body. The only way to shed your inner rigidity is to reconcile yourself to your fate, to stop avoiding everything unknown, troubling, or frightening. Like Jesus Christ, who stands with outstretched arms and invites all those who are rejected by the rest of humankind, we should embrace what troubles us and welcome what's frightening.

For we don't find inner peace by rejecting and repelling but by accepting and integrating—many psychologists subscribe to this view and advise even severely depressed people to treat their depression like an old friend.

The last big goal is to come to an unspoken agreement with the natural conditions of existence, and even more with one's own life in all its aspects, including the bitter and painful ones. Like those two old women in the Italian mountain village, Elisabetta and her friend, who showed every sign of having done this.

Of course it's not easy. It requires insight and persistent practice. But it's somewhat easier if we don't compare ourselves with others. Never mind what's troubling us or what we're lacking—everyone has incomparable value, everyone is to some extent without competition. Avoiding comparing yourself with a sidelong glance to the supposedly enviable—this is liberating, always and everywhere.

If you've gotten this far in life, if you've been a receptive student, then you can face the truth calmly. Are our possibilities really limited? Have they always been? Yes. Just as our self-determination has always been limited. In our mature years, when they arrive, understanding our limits becomes easier. We no longer believe in utopias.

We've learned to accept life—life is too strong, too big. It ridicules our resistance, our precautions, our rebellion. But it's not unfriendly. If we don't resist, it gives us the gifts of wisdom and serenity. Because everything has its time—laughing and crying, building and destroying, fighting and reconciling. And everything needs its time.

12.

The Scary Young

As a young person, one has no idea what it's like to be old. But how is it for old people? Do we have any idea what it's like to be young? Is it easier for us to put ourselves in young people's shoes than vice versa? Are we at all interested in the next generation? An age difference of fifty or sixty years is a lot, and I fear it's hard to bridge the gap in either direction.

Maybe both sides feel equally alienated. Do we elderly shudder at the sight of a group of young people with their provocatively self-confident, vigorous aura, in the same way the fourteen-year-old Maik in Herrndorf's novel did at the sight of the down-at-the-heel, beige travel group of seniors?

Of course we old ones have the advantage of having been young. We know what it was like to be them, while they don't know the same about us. But does that make it easier? It seems we elderly are repelled by the typical characteristics of the young, suspicious of what they take for granted, and uneasy about what they are passionate about, even so. In the end, we have to admit we find young people no less scary than they do us.

That is nothing new. Plato suspected nothing good about young people, and what struck him first was their lack of discipline.

Certainly one envies the young their vitality, the self-confidence they radiate, their nonchalance, their opportunities with the opposite sex—but does one want to be like them? So rude, disrespectful, and inconsiderate, and so ignorant and inexperienced?

Hasn't it always been right for the older citizens to give themselves some credit for their age, precisely because, over the years, they have made the heroic effort of casting aside the errors of their youth? Aren't they right to believe they've earned esteem and respect?

———

The potential for conflict between young and old is real. The Bible contains a dramatic story on this subject. It's found in the second book of Kings, chapter 2: The prophet Elisha has gone bald with age. Is he secretly distressed by this? Of course we don't know, and actually a prophet should be above such trivial things. Yet it seems to have been a weak point, because one day when Elisha is on his travels through the country and passes the town of Bethel, a horde of small boys bursts out of the gate and shouts, "Go away baldhead! Go away baldhead!" whereupon Elisha furiously turns and curses them all in the name of the Almighty. His curse is heard immediately, and two bears come out of the woods and maul forty-two of the boys.

This band of children easily drove the old man into a rage; it happened quickly, and the same can be true today. Of course, in this story, the disproportion between offense and punishment is disturbing; I'd have been happier if the aged Elisha had acted more calmly. But this little incident—taking up no more than two verses in the Bible—makes abundantly clear what's at stake in the relationship between young and old: it's about order and submission, power and veneration.

This story shows what is in actual fact our weakest point as older people. We're sensitive and vulnerable because we still have something to lose: our power—our control over those who follow in our wake, the young, this next generation that makes us uneasy. Inevitably, the relationship between the generations thus always bears the marks of a power struggle.

It's true that in our latitudes, control is actually in decline today. A few decades ago, we experienced an antiauthoritarian revolution, and ever since then the older age groups no longer hold claim to power the way they used to. This might be why the Elisha story simply looks cruel to us. A reader at the time the text was written would, however, have understood this text quite differently—namely, as an urgent warning not to treat old people in such an offensive way.

The situation was clear then: the old people had the say; the young had to submit to them and wait their turn. And as strange as this simple formula for the generational conflict may appear to us in the West today, in many parts of the world, it remains how society functions. I experience it on my journeys abroad. In Africa and Asia in particular, age is valued much more highly than it is in the West. There, the old have a far higher standing than the young and because of this standing can have a much greater effect on the society.

In the countries of the Far East dominated by the influence of Confucius, people today certainly would still understand the wrath of the prophet Elisha. The unwritten laws of this culture require that a young person offer his seat on public transport to an older one without being asked; if he refuses to do so, his behavior could unleash a scandal that is reported in the press, as happened recently in China. In South Korea, where I've made many trips, the word of an old person almost has the force of law even now, in spite of the democratic conditions and the Americanization of large areas of life.

It's no different in Africa. A person whose skills and qualities have reached full maturity in the course of his life and who therefore ranks as a wise old man has supreme authority as the family or clan chief. There is a special word for these venerable old people in Africa, *mzee*, an honorary title I heard on one of my first trips to Africa. My African confreres picked me up at the airport in Dar es Salaam, Tanzania, and on the long drive inland stopped for a picnic.

I was walking around stretching my legs when I heard one of them say, "Give the *mzee* over there something to eat too." Because I was not yet familiar with the customs in Africa, it sounded like "Give the *old man* over there something to eat too." As the relatively young archabbot of St. Ottilien at the time, it took me somewhat by surprise. In reality, *mzee* is an expression of respect and was an extreme compliment, bearing in mind what happened to me on my first visit to Tanzania.

I was thirty-eight when I made my first visit to a convent of sisters in southeastern Tanzania, and when I went to my car after saying goodbye, the sisters flocked after me like a swarm of bees, flitting between the trees, pointing repeatedly at me, giggling and saying *Kijana, kijana*, which roughly translates as, "Look at that spring chicken." A thirty-eight-year-old, and on top of that rather slightly built, in a leading position? It just didn't add up. *He is far too immature—and too thin!* they were thinking.

In Africa, you have to be advanced in years and portly to qualify for leadership, as in Europe it helps to have a long black, or best of all a gray, beard. It regularly creates problems in African monasteries when a younger man is elected abbot. He simply cannot project authority.

Actually at the time, I did feel too young. In St. Ottilien we had a tradition of commissioning an oil painting of each archabbot. At thirty-seven, when my portrait was finished, I was unexpectedly disappointed. What a young face! A face without wrinkles and furrows; a face on which life had as yet left no traces. This was supposed to be an abbot? Alongside the portraits of other archabbots, all fairly old and definitely venerable, I looked thoroughly inconsequential. When I look at this portrait now, I wonder if it's really me.

When I became abbot primate, my successor archabbot, Jeremias, saw the problem and sent a painter to Rome for a second attempt. The new painting now hangs in our refectory alongside those of my predecessors. I always sit with my back to it—but at least the person portrayed undoubtedly looks like an abbot, or for that matter like an abbot primate.

It wasn't easy for me when I became archabbot in St. Ottilien as a "youngster." You can imagine what it was like with my confreres suddenly having to call me "Father Archabbot." Some older monks had difficulty bringing themselves to say these two words, and I felt a bit strange with it myself.

Prior Paul solved the problem in his own way. He didn't hesitate to call me "Most Reverend Father"—the quietly ironic undertone probably making it easier for him to address a person thirty years younger with the required respect. It was Paul who put an end to the unusual generational conflict. He said firmly, "The man has been lawfully elected, so he's our archabbot," and the matter was settled at St. Ottilien once and for all.

But the authority inherent in an office isn't everything. Something else is necessary, something that can't be faked: natural authority. This develops gradually; it takes time.

It may be surprising, actually, that even today, age can have a strange aura, an aura of authority. Young people have a certain fascination with it, and sometimes concede the edge with respect to knowledge, experience, credibility, and trustworthiness, without requiring evidence, to an older person. As long, it has to be said, as the older person in question doesn't give the impression of being helpless or become ridiculous through ingratiating behavior. In all other cases, however, authority comes automatically with age.

As an older person, you can't help it. Authority more or less arrives with gray hair, and it happily makes up for one of the deficiencies of age: it gives us an assertiveness we'd otherwise lose along with our waning physical strength and youthful charm.

This natural authority of age that reinforces what we say and increases over time is a great advantage of age and a very precious treasure. Is the respect of younger people mixed with a little compassion? A little mercy? As far as I'm concerned, this shouldn't bother us. It's rather a question of how we use this authority in relation to younger people, to prevent a power struggle from developing.

St. Ottilien is a good example of how to do this. In the 1960s, the old and the young here got along pretty well. The long-established confreres who kept the huge abbey going, in particular, were on the whole good-natured and open-minded in their dealings with us youngsters.

I remember particularly well the aged Father Alkuin, who encouraged me to take up the flute again, which I'd neglected. On the occasion of the "Monastery Days," young people from outside regularly came to St. Ottilien, and then you could see Father Alkuin sitting with them at breakfast, always curious, always interested in what they were talking about.

When scouts were camping nearby, a somewhat eccentric confrere went to talk to them and kept producing rolls and apples out of his huge bag. In St. Ottilien, we had these old people who simply had nothing but goodwill toward the young; by showing me that they, the elderly, didn't need to act superior to the young, I, one of the young, didn't need to act superior to the old.

Incidentally, their behavior was quite in the spirit of St. Benedict, who takes a positively antiauthoritarian tone in his monastic Rule. Let's look at two places where he explicitly deals with the relationship between young and old.

The first says, "The old should love the young and the young should respect the old." The second deals with democracy in a monastery, and here it says, "As often as anything important is to be done, the abbot shall call the whole community. . . . The reason why we have said all should be called for counsel is that the Lord often reveals what is better to the younger." Two astonishing statements, written at a time when the reputation of a person in society depended on his age, and a young person had little say outside the monastery.

Here Benedict reminds his older monks of a timeless truth. If you're benevolent toward the young and also take them just as seriously as your peers, then they will also respect you—which is actually the basic principle governing relationships between young and old. And I'm sure anyone who takes this to heart will neither need to put on a show of force nor experience major power struggles.

Because actually, young people like listening to their wise elders. They're even positively grateful for such opportunities. We can offer them something fascinating—namely, a spiritual world beyond the trends and fashions they're often trapped in themselves, an independent, free way of thinking based on experience, a different kind of seriousness, a different kind of humor, and new perspectives, new horizons.

The fact that we don't confuse passing fads with eternal truths is precisely our strength. We don't have to take current trends into account, don't have to fit into any scheme, so we're unconventional, independent, and no longer seeking approval.

This means we can take conversations in completely unexpected directions. It also means we can possibly cause offense. So what? One young person may turn away from us shaking his head. But another will feel with growing enthusiasm that a new unknown world is opening up, and some things in his or her world will suddenly look completely different.

And who knows—perhaps a younger person will ultimately think that God sometimes reveals what's right to the elderly too.

13.

Honor Your Father and Mother

Is my picture of young people too rosy? Sometimes we old people ask ourselves whether we can still expect to be taken seriously by them at all or whether they see us as so outdated that our views are no longer relevant. I do think it is getting more difficult. Listening seems to be a lost art for the Facebook generation. It's not that they don't want to listen. But people have put themselves in a state of artificial deafness; they are simply no longer able to listen and as a result become blind to any other world outside their own. There is a very real tendency for people to isolate or cocoon themselves in a digital parallel world, and I'm suspicious of it.

On the other hand, is my picture of old people perhaps also too rosy? Isn't it true that old people have all kinds of quirks and peculiarities that imprison them in a comparably unreal parallel world? I'm not talking about habits. Going to a bar in the late morning for a glass of wine, as older men here in Italy do, is a fine thing. And a reduced sense of reality is probably inevitable in old age, because no one can keep up with the breakneck pace at which the real world is proceeding. But often old people stubbornly barricade themselves in a world of memories.

And there are elderly people who act like they know it all. They say, "But back when I was young, *that's* how it was," and "In my day, *that's* how it was done." Others tell you in a tone of excruciating boredom, "I've seen it all. It's all been done before," and "I've been there; I've always known that; I told you." If things like this are said harshly, forget it, no one is going to give such people the time of day. Somewhat older folks might be okay with ignoring such annoying quirks, but with young people this kind of behavior goes down very badly.

And aside from these things, old people are in some ways fundamentally different from young people. I noticed this again when I was spending the evening with all the confreres in a Spanish monastery. An old monk got up in the middle of the conversation and pressed the dimmer to turn down the light. He wanted to save energy. This reminded me of the older confreres at St. Ottilien, who, while you were still sitting in the room, sometimes would switch off the light when they left. Brother Adolf, our porter at St. Ottilien, before a phone call would write down every word of the conversation he was going to have in order to save phone charges—terrified of telephoning for a second longer than necessary! In the age of flat rates and the nonstop use of cell phones, iPhones, and whatever else, this stinginess seems bizarre—something from a long-past age.

But are there not still surprising points in common between old and young? Isn't saving energy a major issue again? Of course young people have grown up thinking everything can be increased and improved without limit, so they're not starting from the same point. But with an earth that no longer has so much to offer, with natural resources that are limited and our need to economize, aren't they then the first to join in enthusiastically with environmental conservation? Perhaps the young lady texting on her cell phone is not so very different from Brother Adolf after all?

And where common ground is lacking, I think we should simply accept each other as we are. Quirks and peculiarities are evenly distributed between young and old. The young pursue label fetishism and dress to extremes, while the old collect porcelain dolls and talk to themselves. (They "go a bit funny," is one way of putting it.)

While the exaggerated behavior of the young might be objected to for their own good, the old should be allowed their eccentricity. The young take the right to do as they please for granted; old people should have the same right. If an elderly mother fills her wardrobe with clothes that are much too young for her, if she spends her money on extravagances or even just wastes it, that's nobody's business, not even her children's.

An old person's own offspring are often the most judgmental. Sons and daughters try to make rules for their elderly parents and prohibit this and that. But who says age obliges you to be reasonable? I fully understand the old lady who said, "I don't have much time left, and I have a lot to catch up on. My entire life I've done what others expected of me, and now that's over, now I'm doing what I want to do." This freedom should be wholeheartedly granted the old after a long, arduous life. Ignore the quirks, and allow them to do as they please—this too is a way of honoring old age.

Conversely, the attitude of old toward young can be a test of patience. It takes a lot of equanimity to say, "Well, in my day it was different, we'd never have done it this way, but if this is how it is today, well, in God's name. . . ."

In any case, it helps ease the tension between generations if we don't make the same assumption as the prophet Elisha that young people are being intentionally malicious, when their behavior is easily explained by nothing but impetuousness and immaturity. I find I admire it when old people seek to understand young people instead of tarring them all with the same brush.

I am reminded of my predecessor at St. Ottilien, Archabbot Suso. When people talk about the shortage of young people in our European monasteries, the usual reasons are immediately trotted out, such as the superficiality and materialism of young people. But with the sharpness of a truly benevolent person, Archabbot Suso turned this around and made everyone see it in an entirely different way.

He said, "I respect young people who enter a monastery nowadays. It was easier for us to do this, because we didn't have much. There wasn't much we had to do without. Those entering a monastery nowadays have to do without infinitely more." *Well*, I thought at the time, *that's an old person who really loves the young the way St. Benedict would expect.*

If you then look more closely at the saint's requirement, you'll make an interesting discovery: Benedict expects significantly more of the older monks than the younger. Showing proper respect for the older monks, as he expects the younger ones to do, is little more than a question of manners; it doesn't require an inner commitment. But loving the young is something else. This genuine, unshakable benevolence is not possible without dedication, true sympathy, and keen involvement. It must be firmly lodged in a person's character. It presupposes a mature personality. It presupposes among other things an ability that I would particularly like to emphasize in this context because, while it is fundamental to all interpersonal relationships, it is especially beneficial in relationships of the old with the young: treating others as equals.

Monks may have it easier at all stages of life because they're not in competition with each other. Outside the monastery, perhaps this ability can only really be developed with advanced age, when competitive thinking is pointless and arrogance is a thing of the past. Finally, you can consider others your equals, regardless of what you used to think of their talents or intellectual abilities. And with this, the temptation to look down arrogantly at young people should also be removed.

We older people shouldn't let all the fight be taken out of us, though. By making ourselves look self-sufficient and despondent, we exclude ourselves from all the livelier areas of life. Contact between the young and the old occurs easily and naturally if we live our lives in a way that looks convincing and inspiring. Recently I spoke to an abbot whose monastery has had no young entrants for a long time.

"I don't know what the reason is," he complained. "Everything's going well with us. We all gather for Divine Office, we have a good liturgy, there is no tension between us, we all get along well together, and still nobody else joins us."

"And what about your enthusiasm?" I asked him. "Do you give people a sense of the joy of monastic life? Only enthusiasm is persuasive."

I admit it's easy for me to talk. My fountain of youth is Sant'Anselmo, the university with its 120 Benedictine students from all over the world.

The best way, probably the only way, to stay young is to be among young people, and sometimes before I even make it to the first Divine Office, standing in the elevator, I find myself with two students, each from a different continent and with a completely different background.

I meet students at the Liturgy of the Hours and at meals, and some ask to speak to me privately. In the company of young people, there's one thing you definitely learn: that there is not just *one* truth and *one* reality. And if you haven't already crossed into a stage of life of wanting nothing but rest and safety, then such encounters will keep you vibrant.

I also am happy to have opportunities to speak to school classes of sixteen- and seventeen-year-olds. Here I often have to bite my tongue. This age group finds the monastic life incomprehensible. They're very interested in sex and extremely skeptical about lifestyles that involve renunciation. I can definitely feel I'm being attacked from the way some questions are formulated, but I have accustomed myself to showing nothing and taking no question personally.

And as soon as these young people notice that they really can ask me anything, and that I am not just telling them what I think they want to hear or embarrassedly offering evasive answers, then they suddenly find it exciting to have somebody from a totally different world, their curiosity prevails, and they listen with concentration.

As in all such situations, I have found that very few people want to listen to advice and that nobody takes you seriously if you act like a know-it-all. But if you speak frankly and modestly about your life and experiences, neither playing the expert nor presenting it as a heroic epic, then you will make contact, and have the opportunity to inspire them.

———◆———

Let's return to that peculiar story about the cursing prophet and the boys and bears. Here a group of adolescents could upset an old man so much with their teasing that he forgot himself and invoked a terrible punishment. How is that possible? The answer is probably this: only a person who is nearing the end of life and who feels the hopelessness shared by all old people through the ages would react like this.

With death ahead of us and the next generation pushing from behind—this is indeed an unpleasant and desperate situation. Not only every cemetery but also every newborn baby reminds us that we're being pushed gradually into the corner. However great the joy over the birth of the first grandchild, it is probably tinged also with sadness. I can't forget the words of an acquaintance and proud grandfather who confessed to me, "The birth of my granddaughter made me feel old for the first time."

Seen from this angle, our position in society isn't an enviable one. It isn't surprising if we now feel helpless. The curse of the prophet is a sign of weakness. A confession of his vulnerability, which is our vulnerability too.

We would welcome it, then, if this impetuous generation incessantly pressing at our heels didn't constantly remind us of our precarious situation. If instead it had the kindness to treat us with a certain sensitivity, or to honor us as it is written in the fourth of the Ten Commandments.

"Honor your father and mother." These are the words of the earliest-known instruction in our culture as to how the young and old should relate to each other. That it's necessary to remind people of this at all says a great deal—evidently the energetic, vigorous younger generations never think much about their predecessors. Perhaps the slight unease we feel at the sight of them is not without reason.

The fourth commandment in any case reminds us of a harsh reality: it's the old who need the most protection—they are gradually being displaced by the young, their strength is steadily decreasing, and they are fighting a losing battle; they are the most vulnerable members of society.

But that was in rural or nomadic society, in which the older people—as useless consumers of the food supply—were a burden to the younger ones. Everything has changed. We no longer live in such a world. Old people today are more self-reliant and able-bodied. So we shouldn't need to insist on honoring them to maintain peace. The fundamental problem of age that remains to this day is that sooner or later we have to request a certain amount of consideration not only because of our decreased strength but also because of our psychological vulnerability. So if it's no longer appropriate to honor the old, perhaps at least we can insist it's appropriate to love them.

A few years ago in Sri Lanka I saw how this might be done. In four places there, Benedictine sisters take care of old people, most of whom are helpless. I visited one of these communities and met thirteen young sisters, who clearly derived great joy from taking care of fifteen very old men and women.

I talked to some of the old women, who'd gone through a great deal in their lives. They'd all brought up children, often not knowing how they would feed them the next day. These old people had earned a dignified retirement and had accepted the help of the sisters gratefully and happily. Undoubtedly there in Sri Lanka, these fathers and mothers were honored, but it wasn't just that. In addition, they were being allowed to feel loved.

14.

My Hairdresser and Pope Francis

People say Mother Teresa was nothing special as a young nun. She had a cheerful temperament, was meek and totally inconspicuous. Then, at the age of thirty-eight, this ordinary, inconspicuous nun went to Calcutta, founded a convent, took care of the dying and lepers for almost fifty years, received the Nobel Peace Prize, and died at eighty-seven a greatly revered and a highly controversial figure. She now has been canonized a saint.

I like people who have nothing special about them. I value them highly. I think it's precisely that which makes them special: their dislike of fuss, their unpretentiousness, their quiet confidence, and the way they modestly serve a cause; in other words they simply do their work and get on with the task at hand. In a variation on the Beatitudes, I would say special are those who don't consider themselves to be special. These are the people who often demonstrate the most amazing qualities. The first person who occurs to me in this respect is my hairdresser in the Testaccio district.

He's about seventy-five. He's not an artist. I don't need one anyway because my hair is only there to protect my head from the tropical sun if I've forgotten my hat (which is why I'm glad I've still got some).

But he does his job well. I'm not afraid to make an appearance anywhere with his haircut. And that would be enough for me. But I have another reason to remain loyal to him. I like his nature. He lets nothing upset him.

He's had no luck with his son, a lazy and ill-tempered fellow who's been unemployed for a long time. But I've never heard him arguing with his son—even then, he's as composed as with everyone else. He is this way every day at his shop; only a small number of the people who populate it have come for a haircut. The rest have come to chat or talk politics.

Recently someone came in who immediately started grumbling on and on—a pensioner from the neighborhood. Essentially, his tirade was about the long waiting times in the registration office, but gradually this spread to his dissatisfaction with a host of other things. *What an unpleasant person*, I thought, but my hairdresser let him talk. Occasionally he nodded his head, sometimes he gave a brief answer, and all the time he calmly continued to work.

"He always grumbles like that," he said to me when the angry old man had finally left. So, he'd already had this a number of times, and I would have thought he'd be fed up with it. It wasn't so. He didn't cut him off; he didn't ignore him; and he took his complaint about the registration office seriously and responded. "You are a pensioner; you have time," he interrupted. "What are you getting annoyed about? The deadline's not until two days' time, so go on. They might have something for you." Even for such an awkward person, he still had a friendly word and good advice.

I was impressed by his enlightened kindness, by the way he naturally and as a matter of course showed himself to be a friend to this notorious complainer. Incidentally, his parting words to the complainer were, "If you haven't been there by the day after tomorrow, then you needn't show your face here again." This warning wasn't meant unkindly either, but as an additional spur.

And so, with my hairdresser everyone finds what they are looking for—whether it's a sympathetic ear, a piece of good advice, or the necessary kick in the pants. With his modest and patient nature, this man does me good every time.

No, I don't like a fuss, especially with regard to myself. I would like to get on with my work, like my hairdresser. And like him, I try to have a sympathetic ear for everyone. If people think this is the case, then I'm satisfied.

So I'm not at all thrilled by the idea of people now wanting to write my biography. "Not in my lifetime," I say—for me the big celebrations of every significant birthday already go against the grain.

(Although, I must admit I have fond memories of my sixty-fifth birthday in St. Ottilien, because Archabbot Jeremias rather cleverly engineered it as a big musical event. I was kept busy on the day; first I played the flute solo in Ravel's "Bolero" with the orchestra; then I conducted the school orchestra; after that I gave a little flute concert together with Mrs. Stampfl; and finally I played rock music with my band, with virtually no time between. Our students had great fun suddenly starting the smoke machine during the rock performance, to the considerable alarm of the abbots in the first rows. I must admit it was a successful celebration.)

Whoever holds high office for a long period of time has to put up with quite a lot. With a little humor, it's usually bearable, even if you attach no importance to honors. Sometimes I have to intervene when something goes too far, as for example with the matter of the plaque—which was certainly well intentioned, but flattery is something I can't abide.

This is what happened: After our monastery shop at Sant'Anselmo had been renovated and redesigned, somebody had the idea of putting up a plaque in honor of my service as renovator of Sant'Anselmo. I strictly forbade it. Nobody's going to put up a monument to me. Was I going to have to pass by my own memorial plaque for the rest of my time in Rome?

I don't like people who trumpet their successes and certainly don't want to be one of them. In the first place, everything I might pride myself on is in reality the result of a huge joint effort—the remodeling work in any case—and second, my tribute is the people who like Sant'Anselmo's new look, and feel good there. I remember only too well the overturned Mao statues in China. If there's no plaque, it won't have to be unscrewed later on. Anyway, as I said, I detest all fuss—even if my talk-show appearances on television might make some people think otherwise.

There are two role models I have in Rome with respect to modesty—two popes, namely, the previous and the current one. Although neither is the type who was never seen as anything special—Benedict XVI in particular drew attention to himself at an early age—as far as their fundamental attitudes are concerned, they are kindred spirits.

Both of them have great personal modesty and a simple, kind approach to other people; in addition, both have put themselves fully in the service of the Church, guided in this by ideas of renewal. While Benedict focused more on the renewal of faith, Francis's mission is more renewal of the Church. (Popes with an exalted air seem to be a thing of the past, incidentally, because even their predecessors had this winning, unpretentious, and loveable way about them.)

People might feel more affinity with Francis than Benedict, with his practical attitude to life. On Francis's first visit to Sant'Anselmo, he surprised me with his realism. It was Ash Wednesday, when we were to go in a procession from here to Santa Sabina. When he said he'd never been to Sant'Anselmo, I gave him a short introduction to our monastery.

I mentioned the 120 monks from forty nations who live with us, and Francis promptly wanted to know, "How on earth do you feed them?"

"Our refectory is big enough," I replied, but apparently I'd misunderstood him because with his thumb and index finger he made the gesture of counting money. So what he really wanted to know was who's paying for their stay in Rome—a very justified question, but an unusual one for a pope.

"They have to pay something themselves," I responded, "and the rest I have to beg." My answer seemed to please him as much as his question had me, because he burst out laughing.

But Pope Benedict certainly could win people over too, with his simple, sincere manner. A prime example of this is his visit to England in 2010. He was eighty-three, and in the days before his arrival, the way the English public acted, you would have thought they were getting a state visit from a bloodthirsty dictator.

He encountered a wave of furious rejection. Hostile articles about him appeared in the media, and Scotland Yard even arrested six men who'd apparently planned to attack him. Benedict didn't let himself be deterred. He traveled to London in spite of this, and a small miracle happened: the protests against his visit were silenced when the English saw him in person.

And this happened even though the pope stood firmly by his convictions, calling on eighty thousand pilgrims in Hyde Park to profess their faith in Jesus Christ even at the risk of being made to look ridiculous. Later he met abuse victims. He asked for their forgiveness and took more time for these meetings than for his discussion with the prime minister. After that, no one doubted his sincerity—one of those present reported afterward that the pope had tears in his eyes.

Finally, during a Mass, Benedict made mention of the German air raids on England in World War II. "Ashamed and horrified," he regretted the suffering inflicted on the inhabitants of English cities through the German bombing. And at some point during his visit the mood changed. First the pope won over the young people in England. Then the crowds cheered him in rainy Birmingham.

And in the end the English media were forced to concede that Benedict XVI is not a Rottweiler after all—more a "saintly grandfather." That was something at least. In any case, in a short time opponents had become admirers.

A man without presumption or bravado—that is also my experience of this pope. He could be gruff, as he demonstrated a few times when he was Cardinal Ratzinger, but as a person there was nothing conceited about him; he was authentic, unwavering, composed, modest, and devoted to his task—rather like my hairdresser (but with a much more difficult mission).

One thing he couldn't do was put his intellectual light under a bushel. It's true that Benedict spoke as he thought, but unfortunately this wasn't in the language of his contemporaries, which constantly led to misunderstandings. His successor, Pope Francis, at least has nothing to worry about on that score.

Francis demonstrates daily that faith can be formulated in a people-friendly way, simply and understandably. His morning sermons are a miracle of clarity—when I saw the first printed versions, I could hardly believe my eyes. He eschewed the quotations from Augustine of his predecessor, which nobody understood anyway, and suddenly the

Christian message sounds fresh, powerful, and convincing from the mouth of a pope.

A person who speaks like this is displaying extreme modesty and also great love—the language of love is after all always simple language. Allied with this is the impression Francis gives that he's not the slightest bit interested in power. It's not just that he places no value on all the religious pomp, but that he also demands no special treatment.

I have a photo of Francis being blessed by the head of the Anglican Communion. For some this is apostasy taken to extremes, but I imagine he's set a few things in motion with this attitude. If power is no longer an issue, people will perhaps listen to the Christian message again instead of gazing hypnotically at this institution of the Church, which appears to be so power-conscious. And when somebody also speaks in such a way that you enjoy listening to him, well . . .

So here is a man in his late seventies as a bearer of hope, a reformer! Who would have thought it? He's even a daredevil! Or what other word is there for somebody who threatens the Mafia with excommunication, well knowing what he risks? He's making powerful enemies. Would a younger person have such courage?

On top of this, Francis is reviving the discussion within the Church about marriage and family. He wants the changed realities of life to be taken into account. Although this is long overdue, it's perhaps an even braver move than confronting the Mafia. There's no question something has to be done in this area. For a long time it has bothered me that, for example, the Church sees the remarriage of divorced people mainly in the light of sexual desire, but apparently doesn't care at all about the psychological consequences of a broken marriage— also for the children!

What is the message of the Church? Compassion. So how can it be so unmerciful as to generally assume that remarried people are living in a state of sin? Francis, the man from Buenos Aires, seems to be of the same opinion.

I find that a pope who has a sound understanding not only of theology but also of life is a blessing. Anyway, I see the importance of theology declining because most people are totally indifferent to its subtleties and differentiations. Christendom will merge for the simple reason that the differences between the denominations have been forgotten. The time of theological dispute is finally over. I consider Francis to be on the right path when he summons all of us to bear witness together to the love of God and Jesus Christ.

And he doesn't restrict himself to summoning us; he acts. I remember his attempt to prevent the war in Syria in 2012. The efforts of John Paul II to prevent the war in Iraq by diplomatic means failed; Francis tackled the problem from the spiritual side and proclaimed a day of prayer and fasting for peace in Syria.

On this day houses of worship were full around the globe, not just the Catholic churches, but also the Protestant and Anglican ones and even the mosques: a real gathering of all people of goodwill across denominations and religions. Even though the effect might not be noticeable yet, awareness of a common responsibility for peace has grown, and, who knows, this precise fact could prove crucial.

And then came the next step: a joint prayer for peace in Rome with Israeli president Shimon Peres and Palestinian president Mahmoud Abbas. When Francis suggested this during his visit to Israel in 2014, I was in Jerusalem as a co-commentator for the German broadcasting company ARD. I couldn't believe my ears. A Muslim, a Jew, and a Christian united in prayer? Standing with bowed heads before their God? I found the idea incredibly bold and almost too good to be true.

Here was someone who was really treading a new path. I had to search for words myself before I could explain to the reporter that

Francis looks at politics from the point of view of the Gospel. This is a new approach. The peace that comes from God is a gift of grace, and this gift must be solicited with humility and trust in God. Unlike the external peace of diplomacy, the divine peace transforms human beings from within.

Pope Francis may believe people are unable to remain enemies after entrusting their common concern to God. I imagine that the confidence in their faith these three men publicly demonstrated has stimulated the peace negotiations in a way diplomatic initiatives never could.

So here we have a pope who doesn't need to make major proclamations or spectacular gestures; and for precisely this reason he embodies a practical, lively form of Christianity. Christianity like this always has a liberating and thrilling impact, and suddenly there's new hope for us all.

But I'm also full of admiration for his predecessor Benedict XVI. His retirement was a sovereign decision taken with the wisdom of age— nobody forced him to it, as the media has speculated. With the condition of the Church and the time and energy needed, it was simply too much for him—he wasn't strong enough for it. Always personally unassuming, he withdrew to a small monastery convent in the Vatican—and he has resisted the obvious temptation to continue writing books, in order not to question the authority of the current pope. It is also worth noting that after such a fruitful life, it would have been hard not to succumb to the illusion of being irreplaceable, but instead to humbly enjoy one's deserved rest.

Three old men. My hairdresser and two popes, each of them an example of benevolence. None of them disadvantaged by age—because you have the greatest impact when you stop wanting to be someone special and you subordinate yourself to your task. It's much easier to stop posing as a hero and savior when you're old than when you're young. Vanity is no longer a temptation, which makes it easier to concentrate on what's essential. And last but not least, these three people show the composure characteristic of psychological maturity. How different these men would be if those qualities were replaced by trendy attitudes and outfits, youthful slang and lax manners.

15.

On the Brevity of Life

If we make a list of what's wrong with life, what's right at the top? Probably two things: it's too short, and it ends pitifully.

The pictures speak for themselves. Even if we don't look for old people, they impress themselves on us: the old man shuffling along the sidewalk with his walker, the old lady in a café groping with a shaking hand for her coffee cup. Half a dozen loony old people sitting around a big table somewhere in a home. Such images stick in our minds and confirm our worst fears.

A quick, sudden death is maybe not the worst thing that could happen. It is shocking for other people but spares you from what you least want—a final period with torment, suffering that may start somewhere around your eighty-fifth birthday if not earlier. (As an old lady said, "Dying isn't so bad, but suffering?") I'm not sure that images of frailty have been piling up because people in our part of the world have started to live longer; in countries with lower life expectancies, you see even more misery.

But what is definitely increasing is the number of old or very old people you see on the street. They can't be overlooked; they are constantly before our eyes, making us wonder: *Will the deterioration be as clearly written all over my face when I'm their age? Can I avoid the brutal devastation of the body? Can we at least postpone the inevitable and mitigate its consequences?*

And the likelihood of reaching a great age is only increasing. I've read that every second baby born today can expect a life span of a hundred years. Is this a happy prospect?

Delightful and disturbing at the same time, perhaps. Although we want a long life—we still wish this for even the oldest people every birthday—we want to complete these eighty, ninety, or (in future even) one hundred years in halfway decent condition. And so we have to do something about it. We don't want to count on good luck, nor can we.

My impression is that more and more people start thinking about their bodies when they pass the magic threshold of their sixtieth birthday—less to preserve their beauty and youth than their health. And that's a very good thing.

Not that I'm an expert on this matter, but there are two things I find plausible and reasonable: exercise more—move the body more—and pay attention to nutrition.

Nothing seems to be more damaging to our health than a sedentary way of life. The development of technologies designed to make life easier and more comfortable are only making us increasingly lazy. Jogging, walking, and all kinds of sport and fitness training address this. If you make a pilgrimage, because of the goal in mind, you will find a degree of stamina you'd never have thought possible. Many people are active in one of these ways.

It's clear to me that I also sit too much, on planes for example. And I don't jog or go to a gym. My morning stretching exercises wake me up after a short night's sleep, and the monastic life inherently involves movement. The Liturgy of the Hours five times a day is part of the daily routine—each time, I interrupt my work and walk to the church, spend a quarter of an hour or more standing and singing, then walk back again. Singing is doubly beneficial to health because it does both body and soul good. Then there's my favorite walk in the airport—from one gate to the next or from the plane to the baggage claim—and that's all the physical exercise I have time for.

I'm fascinated by another way of countering premature aging that is gaining ground rapidly in Germany (less so in Italy): changing one's diet according to the latest medical findings. In my experience it's usually women who make drastic changes and bring their hesitant or even resistant husbands along with no choice. Gently but firmly and with lengthy reasoning, they persuade their men to abandon old food habits and subject themselves to a culinary regime that places health before taste and enjoyment.

All the easier if what comes out of the mixer, contrary to expectations, doesn't taste that bad—for example, a smoothie of spinach, beet, pears, and bananas. Even nettle salad is now acceptable, because people know its nutritional value.

Fifty percent of what you eat every day should be raw, and of this, 50 percent should be green, because the composition of chlorophyll corresponds 90 percent to that of our blood. And it's best to eat no meat; but if you do, more white than red, and fish is preferable to any meat.

Is this the right way to go? I can't say. But from all I hear, consciously following a diet of this kind increases your physical well-being. You feel lighter, people say, full of energy, and therefore, also, younger.

As a half-Roman, however, I swear more by the Italian formula: if it tastes good, it's healthy, and joie de vivre is the best life insurance. That's why I stick with our excellent Sant'Anselmo monastery cuisine, but in smaller quantities, as I've said before. (The Italian diet is innately natural, and thus easy to digest.)

If you exercise and eat sensibly, you'll certainly be more robust and less prone to illness, and so you'll stay healthy longer. There's no remedy, though, for the other main complaint about old age: that time seems to pass faster and faster and life feels shorter than it should be.

Everybody who's reached a certain age is familiar with this strange phenomenon: *When was the last Deep Purple concert at Benediktbeuern? Two years ago?* I ask myself. I look it up, and lo and behold, it was five years ago! Time flies by and years pass without our registering them. It's frightening, because this means the fifteen or twenty years I still have, perhaps, will seem like seven or eight. If time accelerates at the same rate as in the past, they might even seem like only four or five!

In other words, our stock of time is diminishing, and that's worrying. The days don't get shorter, but the months and the years do, and every new year is shorter than the previous one. You feel downright cheated of your time—ten years are not the same for an old person as for a young one. What do a dozen years mean if they rush past us, if the slope leading into the maw of death gets steeper and steeper and we're tumbling down it headfirst?

We're not yet tired of life. On the contrary, we've got plans, wishes, and hopes, and our greed for life may have subsided, but our appetite for life has not. As far as we're concerned, it could go on for quite a while longer like this. The previously quoted author Sibylle Berg says she thinks it would be great to live for five hundred years, and she dreams of scientific progress that would make it possible one day.

But then you think again. Five hundred years? On what planet would you have to live not to be consigned to the scrap heap for the last three hundred? Here, young people consider even forty-year-olds to be over the hill. And if the body could cope with the exertions of a five-hundred-year life, what about the psyche? Could it process the experiences of a life span equivalent to the period from Columbus's arrival in America to the moon landing by Americans? You only feel comfortable when you can understand what's going on. Could a person avoid getting thoroughly tired with such a long life?

Poetry addresses the topic in the form of the Wandering Jew, a human being who's not allowed to die and longs for nothing more than death. The greatest curse of this endlessly protracted life is the restlessness, the homelessness, the unbridgeable alienation from a world in which he's already lost interest. This even now awaits those who hold out longer in this world than the usual eighty or ninety years. Five hundred? For me in any case it's one of the nightmares created by the belief that everything is technically feasible.

<hr />

On the other hand, Methuselah would have laughed at 500 years. He was almost twice that old, dying at 969. Of course, this was a long time ago. Methuselah was one of the eight forefathers of humankind from Adam to Noah who are listed in the fifth chapter of Genesis, and he's by no means the only one to reach such an age, as more than 900 years of life are also given to most of the others on the list. The proverbial "biblical age" relates to this group of eight forefathers. So was there actually once a life expectancy that exceeds our wildest hopes?

No, certainly not. The entire passage belongs to that part of the Old Testament shrouded in the mists of mystical prehistory, and neither the people nor their ages are historically accurate as we would understand it. We can only guess at how these life spans were arrived at; but this Scripture also says all eight forefathers were between 60 and 120 when they had their first sons, so that tells us a different way of counting must be at play.

What's probably going on here is a glorified approach to the far distant past—making it greater and more illustrious than it was. At any rate, even a literal reading of the Bible will not give us hope God has ever fulfilled the dream of a 1,000-year life span.

I find this great age less interesting than the fact that these ages that extend into historical time are given at all. After the Flood, more realistic life spans soon become the norm. Noah, who survived the Flood with his family as the representative of legendary prehistory, lives for 950 years, but Abraham dies at 175, the patriarch Jacob at 147, and Moses at 120. That's still a lot, and is probably to be understood as showing divine favor of these men; but with Moses's 120 years, we enter the realm of the biologically possible.

Today, scientists consider 120 years to be the upper limit achievable by a human organism without being in a state of permanent repair. This estimate is confirmed by experience: as far as I know, the Frenchwoman Marie Bremont with her 115 years achieved the oldest age of all time. So it's amazing to come upon the statement early in Genesis, in the sixth chapter, that God decided before the Flood to limit the age of humankind to 120 years.

This passage must have been written around 2,500 years ago. Apparently it had already been observed that this was something of an absolute limit, which in turn is evidence for the fact that there must have been 120-year-olds in ancient times. A fairly reliable limit is thus set to our hope of a long life: 120 and that's it—assuming you don't want to exist as a set of prostheses for the rest of your life.

Some imagine this alternate scenario, thanks to this era of technical advancements: visions of a future human being whose organs and limbs are high-tech prostheses, more powerful and durable than those of flesh and blood. But who would seriously want that? Would anyone want—whether with a natural or technically enhanced constitution—to outlive the full span of 120 years?

Wouldn't the vast majority say, "That's enough!" before this? Not just because frailty has robbed them of their vital energy, but because the capacity of the mind to take in any more is exhausted—because it's full to bursting with joyful and painful life experiences? Or, along with the high-performance medical advances of our day, will ways be found to increase the mind's ability to accommodate more experience, or even abolish this ability altogether?

———•◦•———

The Old Testament in any case values great age not for the sheer length of life but for its fullness, its abundant wisdom and experience accumulated during an eventful life history shaped with energy and intelligence. A good death is then one that comes easily because the person concerned has fully exploited her opportunities, has used her abilities to the extent that she has no more hunger for life.

Someone like this says goodbye like a guest leaving the house of his host, satisfied after a big, delicious meal. It is said of Abraham briefly that he joined his forefathers in a good age and full of years, and of King David, in a little more detail, that he died full of days, riches, and honor.

Scripture says a second factor is required to make a life happy and successful: biological fertility. One is fulfilled not just through personal successes but also through giving life to new citizens of the earth who grow up and have their own successes. A tribute to Job at the end of the book named after him expresses the happiness of having numerous progeny in a virtually exultant tone: "He also had seven sons and three daughters. . . . In all the land there were no women so beautiful as Job's daughters. . . . After this Job lived one hundred and forty years, and saw his children, and his children's children, four generations. And Job died, old and full of days" (Job 42:13–17).

In short: what counts is the fertility of a life—fertility in all its connotations, life lived and experienced to the full. It's not a question of intensity or duration; not quantity but rather quality.

The duration of life—the number of years—does play a role, though. An unusually long life is a timeless human desire, so its fulfillment is in the category of happiness in the Bible, and like everything good that happens to one, it is a sign of divine favor, of divine blessing.

There is an Old Testament text attributed to the prophet Isaiah that speaks in moving terms about the happiness of growing old. At the very end of his writings, he envisages a period of divine peace for the city of Jerusalem and in this context alludes to the life expectancy of the residents.

> No more shall the sound of weeping be heard in it,
>> or the cry of distress.
> No more shall there be in it
>> an infant that lives but a few days,
>> or an old person who does not live out a lifetime;
> for one who dies at a hundred years will be considered a youth,
>> and one who falls short of a hundred will be considered accursed. . . .
> They shall not labor in vain,
>> or bear children for calamity,
> for they shall be offspring blessed by the LORD—
>> and their descendants as well. (Isa. 65:19–20, 23)

An age of more than a hundred years as a favor and a gift, as a beautiful accompaniment to a happy and blessed time of peace: this is a dream that was even dreamed by prophets.

16.

A Fulfilled Life

So, I say the prospect of nine hundred, or even five hundred, years of life is undoubtedly ghastly. But the prospect of ninety or a hundred can be no better. I know people whose lives soon after retirement become gray and bland and more like a gradual dying process, not because they are severely ill but because they don't know what to do with their new lives. Weariness and boredom are unwanted but persistent guests, and their lives now revolve around only two things: on the one hand, minor health problems and doctor's visits, and on the other hand, meals.

Should they go out for dinner, or stay at home and cook? If they go out, then where? If they stay at home, what should they have? What does their partner want?

And that's how it is every day. Food is the main topic, unless a dentist's appointment or a colonoscopy is pending. There is nothing in life to give them a purpose or something to talk about. Left to their own devices, they can summon up no particular interest in the world. When it has gotten to this point, it won't be long before mental activity ceases.

Can you really look forward to thirty more years under these circumstances? And would you then take your leave serenely and "full of days"?

Old age as nothing but a tedious intermezzo between working life and death—I hate to think about how many people confuse working and earning money with life, and in the process forget how to live. Their financial situation is fine, but the future looks yawningly empty.

Now, although they have everything, they're left with nothing, because after retirement it's the inner wealth that counts. In old age, the things that translate to wealth are the things you weren't paid for in your professional life. We're living off our psychological savings too, and now we find out whether what we've stored up is really as valuable and durable as we thought, and whether it's what we need to be satisfied with life in the end. Even on the psychological side, it's not the big achievements and heroic deeds that make life fulfilling. It's more the direction and weight we give our life.

That's why my father, for example, could take his leave as calmly as he did. Because he wasn't a hero; he was neither ambitious nor successful. A tailor throughout his life, at seventy-five he was still standing at the ironing machine at a traditional costume company. But he had modest expectations of life, and when I look at the photo that shows him dancing with my mother for the last time—at their golden wedding anniversary—I see a satisfied person.

Many years later I was on the way to Jerusalem and wanted to make a brief stop at my parents' house to say goodbye. My father lay stretched out on the chaise longue, white-haired and almost eighty-six but by no means lacking the strength to carry on, and said, "Well, we won't see each other again."

I didn't quite know what to say.

"Look," he said, "why should I carry on living? I'm already starting to sit around in doctors' offices, nothing's right anymore, and I've done my bit in life. You and your sister can cope. Take care of your mother; my time is over."

I've since met a number of old people who see their death coming; after a life of honest effort, they can leave without regret—my father was one of these.

When I landed at Frankfurt four days later, I called home and was told he'd already died. How you do this, I have no idea. But frankly, I'm not in a hurry to do it myself; and I don't have to know this soon.

———

Is it possible to prepare oneself for dying? Is there a type of courage to die, with which you can arm yourself against the growing fear of death— somewhere between the kind of courage we all share to face life and the supreme variety of the very brave? And if so, what would make you so fulfilled or wise that you could look ahead serenely to your final hour?

Humankind has probably always thought about this. It's a burning question, and there's a well-stocked treasure trove of answers. Reach in, and you'll always take out something wise. When I did this, I came up with three answers from different periods that I would now like to share with you.

The first answer, from Psalm 39, is this:

> Lord, let me know my end,
>> and what is the measure of my days;
>> let me know how fleeting my life is.
> You have made my days a few handbreadths,
>> and my lifetime is as nothing in your sight.
> Surely everyone stands as a mere breath.
>> Surely everyone goes about like a shadow.
> Surely for nothing they are in turmoil,
>> they heap up, and do not know who will gather.
> And now, O Lord, what do I wait for?
>> My hope is in you. (Ps. 39:4–7)

An astonishing text that immediately touches you. Here is someone who, two and a half thousand years ago, forced himself to think about age and dying. Everything in him rebelled against it. He asked God for courage: *Lord, let me know . . . because actually I don't want this, actually I'm afraid. I don't want to know that there's a limit to my life too, this life I cling to.*

I imagine that the writer of this psalm is in the prime of life when he's suddenly seized by the unknown sorrow of parting and boldly turns things around and looks at things from a completely different perspective, from right outside himself. And suddenly he sees with utter clarity that what makes humanity appear so great, important, and unique—namely, life itself—is nothing more than the brief flickering of a flame soon extinguished. All people think they are safe, cling to the illusion that everything's up to them. Looked at from a distance, however, the turbulent theater of humankind is like a ghostly shadow play. And like a shadow, no one leaves a trace. World affairs are all meaningless and in vain.

Is this reassuring? No, it definitely isn't. It is a bitter pill to swallow. But this brutal realism certainly is good for us. It may not reconcile us with the facts, but at least it can familiarize us with them and, quite possibly, facilitate acceptance of the unalterable at the end. Should we be satisfied with this?

The psalmist isn't. He insists on compensation—for having to say farewell forever to a place he liked, to a world that can be so infinitely beautiful, to a life where not all promises have been fulfilled by any means, to people he loves. And he follows his sober assessment with a whispered cry for help: "What do I wait for? My hope is in you."

We're just not realists. We're not satisfied with the loathsome facts. We demand more because we love life, so the psalmist finally arrives at trusting God—God who will do as well by him after death as he has done before—and throws himself into the arms of God. Not that there aren't good reasons to give up hope. There are objective reasons the psalmist doesn't ignore, but they aren't decisive. What decides things is his longing, with which he can turn only to God.

In a way, what we witness in the few verses of this great psalm is an initial act of faith. We understand that the way to faith leads through facing the brutal parts of reality, but we understand also that it means facing up to ourselves and our desire for happiness. This higher realism is faith, and in my experience it is a good preparation for dying.

———◆———

Several centuries after the psalmist, Roman philosopher Seneca wrote an essay in which he dealt with the complaint that life is too short. It's funny to read that the same complaint and reason were given in ancient Rome as now: too much stress, far too much to do. In Seneca's opinion, life is wasted by being uselessly busy. People are immersed in daily business, they never stop and come to their senses, and at the end, they say they never had any time for themselves, that life was too short.

Apparently people in Roman society are totally stressed out—at least in the circles frequented by Seneca, which would have been mainly businesspeople and politicians. As a prime example, he points to the emperor Augustus, who never stopped praying for rest during his lifetime. The words with which the overworked Roman politician keeps himself going also sound very modern: "My sixtieth year shall release me from public duties." In other words, when I retire, I'll finally get to the things I've always wanted to do.

No wonder life seems short to you, Seneca says. It's not the fault of life; it's your fault because even the longest life will seem short if you rush about blindly, tormented by lost time. Or as Seneca elegantly puts it, "Everyone hurries his life on and suffers from a yearning for the future and a weariness of the present."

In other words, you distract yourself with whatever is at hand to avoid thinking about yourself and your destiny, wasting your life until it's too late; when near death, "willy nilly, you must find leisure."

How do you gain time in life? Seneca says life is long for a person who incorporates the past, who takes time to reflect and read, who draws from the great fund of wisdom left by previous generations. This will add a long period to life. Such a person "makes his life long by combining all times into one."

But it's foolish to wait to start until you retire. What was true of pensioners of ancient Rome is true today. They were absorbed by business, and now they get into a hopeless state, because nothing can be done at the last minute, for "it takes the whole of life to learn how to live."

Seneca says whoever learns all their life will have another advantage: they'll die in peace: "The wise man will not hesitate to go to meet death with steady step." With this he summarizes the ideal of Stoic philosophy: being able to live is being able to die.

The Stoic ideal may not be to everyone's taste, nor can it be realized in everyone's life, but it's still remarkable: someone who has gotten the best out of life—namely, a wealth of knowledge and wisdom—someone who has lived sustainably, to use a modern expression—won't feel as if he or she has missed out.

Living the wrong way always leaves wishes unfulfilled; living the right way makes people satisfied—and makes dying all the easier. When Emperor Nero demands that Seneca commit suicide, he accepts his fate uncomplainingly and severs his arteries.

The final answer comes from an unexpected quarter: a figure in a fairytale, Hans in Luck. The fairytale of the same name is one of the most enigmatic handed down by the brothers Grimm, and accordingly has been given many different interpretations, but to my knowledge it has never been explained in terms of growing old and dying. Is this really possible? I'll try.

I'll give a brief summary, even for those familiar with what happens, because my case rests on a few easily overlooked details. As a reward for seven years of loyal service, Hans receives a pumpkin-sized nugget of gold from his master and sets off with it to his mother's house. But the nugget is heavy and becomes troublesome to him, so when a horse dealer passes his way and suggests he exchange the gold for his horse, Hans is relieved and happy to do so. And so it continues. After a while, he's equally dissatisfied with the horse and exchanges it for a cow, the cow in turn for a pig, the pig for a goose, and the goose finally for two millstones. With each exchange, he comes off worse—now he is literally dragging two millstones around instead of a gold nugget—but feels himself lucky.

Within sight of his mother's home, he stops to rest at a well and clumsily drops the millstones into the deep shaft. Now nothing at all remains of his wages, but this does not bother him. Finally completely free, he jumps for joy and sets out on the final leg of his journey, arriving at his mother's house a very happy man.

It's common to think of Hans as a young person. But the fairytale gives us a lot of indications that he is actually at the end of his life. If we assume fairytales are generally to be interpreted symbolically, we shouldn't take either the gold nugget or the seven years literally. Seven as a perfect number suggests a completed cycle, and a pumpkin-sized gold nugget would be far too high a reward for a few years as a journeyman. So, let's assume the figure seven stands for Hans's entire working life, which is now behind him, and the gold is payment for that entire life's work.

Hans has not become a boss or master in his business, but he's comfortable, and now he's setting off on his last journey: to his mother's house, it says in the fairytale, but let's not take *mother* literally either. As is common in fairytales and sagas, *mother* probably represents the earth that will soon receive him back—so, his grave.

It's clear that this, Hans's last journey in life, is a story of liberation. Gradually he lets go of the ballast of worldly possessions—and worldly ideas of happiness. After he's tired of what he has, he is pleased with every exchange; by worldly values, these exchanges are unfavorable, but every time he opts for what he sees as a lesser evil. Finally, when through clumsiness he loses the last of the things that burden him or might bind him to the world, he feels enormous relief, and reaches the house of his mother with no possessions at all; in other words he sinks carefree and without regrets, positively redeemed, into the grave.

This is the art of taking leave, shown to us not by a philosopher, not by a religious man or poet, but through a simple fellow, an everyman— even the name Hans could be symbolic; it's a very common name. With incomparable ease and humor, Hans shows how psychological maturity—the unbending of the character observed by Proust—can emerge through turning the laws of the world on their head.

Because this is exactly what Hans does. It doesn't matter to him that others take him for a fool or laugh at him behind his back; he's guided only by an instinctive wisdom that advises him to play the game of life to the end according to a seemingly absurd rule: less is more.

He outsmarts himself even, turning every loss with sly humor into a gain, but in reality unwaveringly—though perhaps subconsciously— following the principle that freedom is the highest goal and the winner is the one who has nothing at the end.

Perhaps that's the cunning of old age.

The art of taking leave, as I said. And it's certainly not the worst answer to our question of whether we can prepare ourselves for dying. I'm reminded of something I experienced.

An uncle of mine died, and I was unable to find time to go to his funeral. On my next visit home, I saw my aunt, and together we went to the grave. Standing in the cemetery, she broke the silence with, "You know, Werner [my birth name], I'm slowly realizing that everything is only borrowed. What we have isn't ours." This was a new insight for my aunt, which had taken seventy-five years to ripen in her.

17.

A Reply to Seneca

S eneca would probably have looked on me with suspicion. "That person has too much on his plate also," he would have said. "He never stops." That's right.

The fact that an abbot primate has no time to watch television is something I can cope with. I miss out on movies too—except sometimes on a plane. But I greatly regret having equally little time for reading. Unfortunately, it can't be changed—my daytime schedule offers no opportunity to take up a book, and in the evening I do my correspondence (and am glad of every spam email because I can delete it immediately).

Thank God, writing letters goes with listening to music. It goes very well with Beethoven sonatas. It goes wonderfully with Mozart's concerto for harp and flute—composed fourteen days after the death of his mother, but nevertheless pure joy. It goes excellently with the work of Georg Philipp Telemann—I ask myself where the dance-like lightness of his music comes from, when the Baroque era was positively in love with mortality; no coffin without a skull, no tomb without a winged skeleton. It's not at all what I think of as Baroque. But perhaps this cheerfulness is only granted to people who are particularly aware of their mortality.

When I've finished—in other words, when the pile of letters on my desk has perceptibly shrunk—it's long past midnight. Peace and quiet have returned—disturbed at most once by the wailing of fire-engine sirens down on the Via Marmorata (the station is not far from us)—and finally, I can sit and reflect.

Sometimes, then, I'm troubled by thoughts of how I'll stand before God when this life is over. Will I be filled with horror when I'm summoned to turn around and look back at my life? Or I think of a statement made by Cardinal Volk on his eightieth birthday: "I'm always being asked whether I'm afraid of the future. No, not in the slightest— it's only my past that I'm afraid of." So, yes, sometimes at such moments I am tempted look back at my life and take stock. But for that I'd have to sit at my desk and continue fighting against my tiredness, which I no longer have strength to do.

I'm consoled that God will be there and will be merciful to me if I collapse when looking back. And so consoled, I switch off the light, go to bed, and profit from a talent I inherited from my father to be able to sleep wherever I am—on a plane, at a meeting, during a boring sermon, and once even at a concert right in front of the booming organ.

I still need to catch up on rest, leisure, and sleep. (Seneca would have had every reason to be dissatisfied with me.) Otherwise, I don't have any great wishes I'd still like to fulfill. I've seen enough of the world. My first small wish, as crazy as it may sound, is that I'd like to look around Rome. At the end of my period of office, I would like to spend another two months in this city to see what Rome is really like today.

Because I haven't had time to do this. Since I moved to Sant'Anselmo as abbot primate in 2000, I've either seen Rome from a distance, at the top of the Aventine, or driven through its clogged streets to a hospital or a church, ignoring everything else. The Rome I know dates from my time as a student, fifty years ago. Many things will have changed. Also, of course, Rome is inexhaustible. So if my love of this city doesn't lead to my remaining here permanently, I'd at least like to enjoy its beauty and riches once as an observant and grateful guest, carefree and released from all duties.

———

And then I'd like to read—to satisfy my desire for literature. My interest in biographies has grown steadily over the years—the life stories of people who've had an influence on world history, not to venerate them, but because I wonder what personal qualities and character traits enabled them to master their exhausting, overcrowded lives. I'm especially curious about the old Romans, Caesar of course but also Cicero, who like Seneca wrote a book about growing old.

What moved, inspired, and drove these people? What mental and spiritual forces? What were they like when no longer bathed in the light of success? And vice versa. What does the philosophy of Immanuel Kant reveal about the person behind it, for example? What mentality and life experience does it reflect? Philosophy is taught consistently as an abstract system, but isn't there a human being behind it every time, trying with his thoughts to cope with his own life? If Kant, as has been said, was someone you could set your watch by, then let's look at his categorical imperative in the context of his meticulously organized life.

This too is an advantage of age: you get a sense of the personal touch in every work. With all your experiences in the course of a seventy-five-year life, you're not so easily fooled by exalted theories. You see in what people devise the traces of a very particular, unique, and also limited and problematic life.

———

More than my ambition to study, what I most long for is the opportunity at last to enjoy culture in peace, with time to digest it properly. In addition to music, I've always found great pleasure in looking at paintings. Sometimes I succeed in inserting a museum visit between two appointments. I then concentrate on a few paintings.

Once, the director of the museum in Dresden wanted to show me the entire collection. "That's too much," I said. "That would be overwhelming, but could you show me two paintings, the *Sistine Madonna* by Raphael and *The Tribute Money* by Titian?" I'm impressed by the expression on the face of Titian's Jesus. Quietly and determinedly, he looks the Pharisee next to him in the eye, with a closed mouth and steady gaze, and this gaze says everything; you don't have to know how he answered the Pharisee's trick question.

If I have time in Madrid, I look at a few paintings in the Prado by Hieronymus Bosch, Velázquez, and Goya, then I spend longest in front of Dürer's *Adam and Eve*—an unbelievable work. In the Louvre, again I confine myself to four or five paintings: the fresco in the Egypt department where Jesus has his arm around a saint; the *Mona Lisa*; and some Renoirs. Freshest in my mind is the Edvard Munch Museum in Oslo, which is magnificent and depressing at the same time. For me, Munch's *The Scream* is the artistic expression of depression, piercingly loud but inaudible—mute despair—which the painter himself knew only too well.

———•———

What I find surprising is that whether I stand in front of a great work of art or listen to a composition of a great composer, each affects me differently than it did ten or twenty years ago. It speaks a clearer language. Apparently you see and hear in a new way with age. This change happens quite unexpectedly. It doesn't seem to be your doing. Life—the efforts of the past—is simply paying off.

The fact that age brings improvements and enrichment when all you expected was wear and tear is amazing enough, but that this virtually drops in your lap as the mature fruit of life is especially inspiring.

I feel this change in particular when I read the Scriptures. They tell me more than they used to. The Gospels, the Letters—they have been speaking to me so directly it's as if I've gotten closer to Jesus and Paul through my life experience. I feel like I've never sung the Psalms before, even though I ought to know them by heart after fifty years of the Liturgy of the Hours. But that's not the case at all—every verse seems new to me. I encounter familiar territory as if I am setting foot on it for the first time. This really does me good, because as a monk, after all, my response to the question of what makes a life good or bad differs from that of the Stoic philosopher Seneca.

"To attribute to God and not to self whatever good one sees in oneself. But to recognize always that the evil is one's own doing, and to impute it to oneself. To fear the day of judgment. . . . To desire eternal life with all the passion of the spirit, to keep death daily before one's eyes, to know for certain that God sees one everywhere." This is what St. Benedict expects of his monks. He hopes to instill in them a basic attitude—namely, awareness of their responsibility to themselves and others.

No matter how onerous it may be, you can't escape this responsibility, because God will demand accountability. And I think we need to be reminded of this occasionally because examples of seriousness and conscientiousness resulting from responsibility to God are not things we encounter too often in this world. We tend to be irresponsible and have a devil-may-care attitude, so it helps to be brought to our senses by such strong words now and again.

"To keep death daily before one's eyes." There's no special preparation for death in Benedict's Rule, though. Reading on in the Rule of Benedict:

"If you want true and everlasting life, you must guard your tongue against evil and depraved speech," one passage says. And another: "Depart from evil, and do good; seek peace, and pursue it" (Ps. 34:14 KJV). These are not complicated instructions. Obviously, it is good if we stop denigrating others. Honesty, sincerity, truthfulness—with these alone, Benedict says, you will make a substantial contribution to peace. Love of truth is something frequently displayed by Pope Francis when he says we speak badly of others far too much, causing strife and in this way destroying community.

Anyone who takes to heart the general injunctions to depart from evil and do good, to live responsibly for God, and to conscientiously do one's duty is prepared for death.

——◆——

The life of a pastor, a priest, or an abbot, however, involves things that are not common for most people. Illness and death are familiar to me: in a monastery or convent, people of all ages live together, and (while there are no births) there is suffering and death—often after a long life. You can't escape encountering mortality here; even as a novice, a young monk, you witness suffering and death at close quarters.

As archabbot of a large monastery like St. Ottilien, it was my duty to support the dying in their last hour, and if at all possible, I sat with them, held their hand, and accompanied them with my prayers to the threshold of the afterlife. Not only out of a sense of duty—holding the hand of a dying person is the only thing you can still do for him and the only thing he still wants. It's a last favor for someone who is leaving this world, and therefore a simple brotherly duty that I gladly perform.

The same of course applies to the world outside the monastery walls. Since I know a lot of people, many turn to me. They're not always looking for consolation or an answer to one of the questions that torment people after a stroke of bad fate. Sometimes they want nothing in particular. Like a ninety-seven-year-old lady who sends me brief, humorous emails from time to time. We've never met, and I don't know much about her. Her letters, riddled with typos, are surrealistic little works of art. But I always reply, and we've now been acquainted for more than a year.

More often, people write hoping for a pastor who will share their grief and find the right words for them. A good friend recently did this. By chance, I was still at my desk at three in the morning (I had a lot to finish before traveling in the morning because I don't like to leave a pile of unanswered mail behind) when his email reached me.

"My wife," he wrote, "has just passed away in my arms. I've got no one I can tell at this late hour, but I must tell someone."

I knew what misfortune had befallen the two. Her father had died a few months earlier; she'd taken care of him for a long time and hadn't gone on any long trips for his sake, consoled by the thought that after his death she'd make up for it. Then the doctor diagnosed a malignant tumor and gave her a maximum of six months. Now the foreseeable had happened. When the diagnosis was made, I'd written to them both. And now I answered my friend—and not with just a couple of lines.

At such moments, one often struggles desperately against the powerlessness of words, though. Even if they're drawn from considerable experience and firm faith, you feel how little such solace can do against the power of a person's pain. And sometimes no sympathetic word, no well-intentioned advice, can bridge the abyss that yawns between us and a suffering person.

So I prefer to follow the example of Job's friends sometimes. They didn't even try to console him; his misfortune was simply too big for words. Instead, they sat down with him and kept silent; they didn't say a word for seven days. In some situations, visiting a suffering person, listening, and showing you won't abandon your friend is more consoling than any words. You are letting your friend know you'll hold open the door to life until new courage is found. This is the most effective help you can give a desperate, downcast soul who's not even sure he or she wants to return to the world yet.

In other words, nothing against Seneca and the Stoic acceptance of fate, sorrow, and death—his wisdom is exemplary—but sharing the sorrow of another person and shouldering a small part of the other's pain, that requires something different, something more than equanimity and philosophical detachment.

18.

As Long as You've Got Your Health

The dam is still holding. But behind it the water seethes menacingly. Black floodwater pounds against it. How long it will hold? Here and there, it has given way, but the damage can still be repaired. Afterward there's still a period of respite. *Still* . . . this treacherous little word *still*. It multiplies uncontrollably. It seeps into our speech like the water into the dam. You can *still* climb the seventy-six steps to the third floor. You can *still* tolerate two glasses of wine in the evening. You *still* can't complain.

But the doctor's visits are more frequent, and before each visit you're more anxious. So far, you've recovered from each illness and continued with your normal life—used to illness as a brief, annoying interruption of a daily life, a break in the accustomed rhythm. Now, though, you have to prepare yourself for diagnoses that profoundly alter your life—and you slip into the role of an accused person waiting for the verdict: is it the death penalty, a life sentence, or will you get off lightly, with a few years, perhaps on probation? If someone offers the old phrase, "as long as you've got your health," you have to agree, don't you?

As I said, the life cycle—the flourishing and waning of the vital forces—is constantly present in a monastery. Monks are more permanently connected with one another than employees of a company, or even family members, and follow each other's fates over decades until the end. In such a community, we have everything: accidents, illness, long infirmity, and gradual mental decline. And usually our sick, old ones are role models of patience.

But shattering experiences also occur. I remember two good monks who committed suicide during a phase of severe depression.

One difference between a monastery and the world outside is that everyone knows he won't be sent to a home. *The others will look after me. After each hospital stay, I return to my monastery, alive or dead.*

Nuns and monks have always been nurses. The word *sister*, which in German is also used in the nursing community, originates from the nuns who formerly staffed nursing services in hospitals everywhere. Even our founder, Benedict, impressed on his monks that they should look after their sick confreres and ordered them in his Rule "to serve the sick as if they were Christ—also with dedication and without fear or favor. No sick person should feel neglected, no one be left alone with his fear and pain."

In St. Ottilien we came very close to this ideal—among my best memories of the early days in the monastery are the evenings in the infirmary where the confreres often sat together after supper and told stories; we novices gladly joined them.

But Benedict was realistic enough to add that the sick in turn should not make excessive claims; in other words, they shouldn't demand special privileges because of their illness and tyrannize the healthy with their whims.

The service of the sick is already stressful enough, as I know from my own experience. For a long time at St. Ottilien, the confreres used to do night duty in the infirmary in addition to their normal daily workload. That's not possible anymore because, with the number of the old confreres, the number of sick is increasing. We've now employed two laypeople to do the night duty.

Anyway, when I started at St. Ottilien we didn't find the fact of growing old with all its consequences particularly tragic; it was part of everyday life in the monastery. With all you hear and know about Alzheimer's today, you shudder just at the mention of the word, but we novices knew nothing about Alzheimer's in those days. Some of the old confreres were just a bit senile—which was no reason not to play little tricks on them—not, of course, out of spite but with our youthful lack of inhibition. With their strange, whimsical nature, these confused confreres were a test of our ingenuity, and we rose eagerly to the challenge.

Brother Balduin was physically quite fit but mentally no longer at his peak; every afternoon one of us went for a walk with him for half an hour so that he got some fresh air. One day he refused to come with me. I went into his room, and he said, "No, I can't go out today."

"Why not?" I asked.

"Well . . . there's Peter."

Uh oh, what's going on here? I thought. Then I remembered that his given name was Paul. Apparently, he'd given himself a twin brother.

"Where's Peter then?"

He pointed to the mirror.

Ah. What should I do? I looked round the room, and a box of chocolates on the table gave me an idea.

"Let's give Peter the chocolates," I said. "He can eat them. It'll give him something to do, and in the meantime we can both go for a walk."

I put the box of chocolates in front of the mirror so that his new twin brother could easily reach in, and Balduin was satisfied. We went on our walk around the monastery grounds as we did every day. Outwit artfulness with even greater artfulness: this little stratagem I also learned from Prior Paul.

Brother Methodius was also already pretty confused. For a long time he'd been the porter at our study house in Munich where I was a student, but now we had to watch that he didn't wander off. Frequently, with a suitcase packed with underwear, handkerchiefs, undershirt, socks, and a breviary, he would set off "to his brother," he would say. Actually, he should have been sent back to St. Ottilien, but he wouldn't have known his way around there after all his years in Munich.

"Hey, Brother Methodius," I said to him one day when I found him about to set off. "You can't just go away."

"Why not?"

"You've been at the monastery for fifty years; you need special dispensation from Rome!"

"Get away," he replied. "Who's going to bother about a lay brother like me."

He was never at a loss for words, but he was seriously confused. Sometimes when I returned late in the evening from a movie or play, all the windows were brightly lit and Brother Methodius was roaming around the house.

"It's already eleven o'clock, and people are still asleep!" he complained.

I led him to a window and showed him that it was dark outside. "Look, *that's* which eleven o'clock it is."

Then it dawned on him. "Oh no," he groaned. "Am I already that bonkers?"

We brought him to bed, prayed with him, made the sign of the cross on his forehead, and he was happy. Afterward I had to go through the whole house turning off the lights.

There were funny moments and sad moments. Once I drove with Brother Methodius to Pfaffenwinkel, his former home. He wanted to see his parents' graves and his birth house again, but when we got there he didn't recognize anything.

As a young monk, situations like these showed you at close quarters what you could expect in old age, and left you uneasy. On the other hand, I liked the confreres with Alzheimer's, not least because of their good nature. When I suddenly had to brake sharply on the way back from Pfaffenwinkel, Brother Methodius banged his head on the windshield.

"Methodius!" I said, worried. "I hope that wasn't too bad?"

He shook his head. "No, no," he replied unmoved. "I've had worse happen."

———

Monks who fall ill remain in the community, in the same way sick children remain with their family. Everyone is taken care of, and no one has to fear being forgotten or cast out in advanced age. That's certainly a privilege. The community makes it easier to deal with physical decline by maintaining the ties connecting a sick person to the world of the healthy.

The will to live is crucial for recovery, and if disabilities remain, it is put to the test a second time. Encouragement and if necessary a firm talking-to work wonders—as happened, for example, with Father Bernhard, the former principal of our school.

I'd just returned from an East Asia trip. The brother in charge of the sick told me tersely, "Father Bernhard is dying. He's had a stroke and is now lying downstairs in his room." I couldn't believe my ears. *What is he doing in his room if he's had a stroke? Why isn't he in the hospital in Landsberg?* Father Bernhard was only seventy, and I couldn't believe this brother's defeatism.

"Remember in future," I impressed on him, "anyone who has a stroke must be in hospital within an hour. And now please call the ambulance."

There was then no more talk of dying, but Father Bernhard was initially paralyzed on his right side. Thank goodness he didn't remain like that. He cooperated diligently with the physiotherapists, and when he returned to St. Ottilien he was almost completely recovered. But he didn't have full mobility back in his fingers and dragged his right leg, and now he withdrew completely. He slammed the door to life behind him. I learned during a visit that his resignation was rooted in humiliation and shame.

"You know," he said, beginning to cry, "how strict I used to be with my students. And now, look at my handwriting—this scrawl. It looks awful." There was nothing to be done. He couldn't face seeing other people as a disabled person. But then his sister visited him, appealed to his conscience, and gave him a good talking-to, and accomplished with her determination what none of us had: reawakening his will to live.

Father Bernhard came out of his self-imposed exile, prayed and ate again in the community, even took on a job in the library, in time digitizing the entire card index. He was pleasant to everybody (which he hadn't always been in the past).

Nor did his second stroke change this. This time the doctor wanted to let him die in his room, but the same brother from the infirmary wasn't having it, after that experience with the first stroke. Inspired by sacred obedience and stalwart as a soldier, he confronted the doctor and declared, "I've been ordered by the Reverend Father that whenever anyone has a stroke, he has to be sent within the hour to the hospital in Landsberg!"

So Father Bernhard was saved a second time, and all his symptoms disappeared during convalescence, except his earlier difficulty writing and walking. Seventeen years after the brother in the infirmary said he was dying, Father Bernhard died at the age of eighty-six of a heart attack—full of days, it can truly be said.

When I sit at the bedside of a seriously ill person, two sayings come to mind, both very old and both taken from the Christian tradition. *We're only guests in this world*, I say to myself or sometimes even out loud. Or I remember something my patron Notker the Stammerer said in the ninth century.

One day he observed two men working at an extremely dangerous height above a gorge over which they were building a bridge. Spellbound, he watched them working unsecured above the abyss. Notker saw this scene equating to the basic human condition and put it into a song that begins with the words: *In the midst of the life we are in death.*

In the past, the omnipresence of death wasn't an embarrassing secret, so the approach to death was matter-of-fact. You laid out the deceased person at home, washed and prepared the body, and finally joined the funeral procession to the grave. Nowadays we imagine we can avoid or eliminate death in some way. The eternal youth of the Greek gods is still humankind's greatest desire, but now people want this dream to be fulfilled in this world.

Even with test-tube fertilization a selection is made: only optimal embryos survive, and the rest are thrown away, so that no imperfect human being can spoil the earthly paradise later on. It's not even eighty years ago that good and bad genetic material and selection was first talked about, and now we are dominated by the idea of an optimized and perfected humankind, for whom suffering is simply out of the question.

I was impressed all the more by John Paul II, who forced the sight of a frail pope on a world obsessed with strength and health. Many people expected him to retire from view, but he opted for the scandal of public, obvious suffering. He illustrated the common fate of humanity in his own person and in this way opened the eyes of some to the abyss over which we dangle. It was a lesson in realism that can be summed up in Christian terms as "before the resurrection comes the cross."

To be precise, what the frail John Paul II achieved was to embody in his pitiable state one of the main commandments of Christianity, the commandment that has always been symbolized by the crucifix: *You shouldn't look away. Don't turn away. Bear the sight of suffering.*

All of Christendom begins with looking, with a loving gaze, with overcoming the reluctance we understandably feel at the sight of misery. It reminds us only too clearly of our own vulnerability, it horrifies us, so I understand the anger nowadays aroused by the crucifix, the tortured body of the crucified. It's an affront, unbearable with its insistent demand to be looked at, its requirement that you shouldn't turn your eyes away but get used to the sight of suffering, familiarize yourself with it, and arm yourself with the power of love. Because your natural impulse tells you to look away, run away!

Yes, I understand the anger against the crucifix. It's an attack on our peace of mind. It tears us from our dream of a completely renewed world without distress or death. And that's exactly its meaning and purpose. Because what the crucifix teaches us—what the bent, trembling body of the sick pope taught us—is nothing less than the sole known formula for humanity: All the good in this world depends on a willingness to be appealed to and shocked. And for this, first of all, you have to look. And want to look.

⟶•⟵

Incidentally, those who expose themselves to the suffering of others have the most amazing experiences. So often, I make a sick call with the intention of consoling the person concerned, and drive home consoled and reinforced. I remember a young couple whose son was born with a double cleft lip. Operations were required, and by the age of two, the little one had survived them all. Then the parents were hit by the next stroke: the final examination showed their child had leukemia.

I could find no words of consolation. They were now thrown into a constant state of anxiety: Would he survive the radiation treatments at the children's hospital? Did he have a chance at all of surviving?

When the parents were at the end of their rope, I drove the three hundred kilometers from St. Ottilien after work. I didn't have much to say, but I didn't want to abandon them.

So I shared their sorrow silently, and I experienced two incredibly brave people: a boy ill with cancer who never complained, and a mother who sat by his bedside and read him beautiful stories in a firm voice. I just sat there and listened. There was no one for me to console. Instead, I went home consoled after witnessing almost superhuman inner strength.

In fact, illness—like love and faith—is a great and powerful transformer. The crisis a sick person goes through happens simultaneously in the body and the mind, and he or she experiences something amazing. Very few people allow themselves to be defeated by their physical suffering. They counter it with an enormous strength that used to be called patience in suffering. And, strangely enough, most people react this way automatically, even after shattering diagnoses. Instead of panicking, they seem to collect themselves, come as it were to their senses, and, perhaps for the first time in a long while, start thinking more deeply.

Illness is restricting, of course. But that's precisely what seems to do us good. Because you can't put on a mask with illness. Suffering brings out the real human being; no putting on an act, however convincing.

Has the luck of good health meant you've been able to avoid coming to your senses until now? Is the truth about life you've managed to evade until now dawning on you? Is crunch time forcing you to fall back on your spiritual resources? That's what happens. We need a really good reason to force us to take a serious critical look at our life, and the sickbed is a good reason.

"I never had time for my family," a businessman who has suffered a heart attack before fifty tells me. "I was always focused on my career. I should have asked myself long ago what I really wanted. Now, at last, I'm starting to reevaluate and reorganize my life." At such moments, you see the sense of St. Benedict's injunction to keep death daily before your eyes. It will get you to question your way of life repeatedly, and not just in a crisis.

Of course, lengthy, agonizing suffering can wear you down. If there's not the slightest hope of improvement, a person may give up. But even in such cases, I've found that illness is accompanied by a clear-sightedness I can confidently describe as purification. Whether everyone who's close to us will understand is another matter; illness can make you lonely.

It can even make you doubly lonely. For one, you lose friends: this is experienced by everyone with a prolonged illness, and there are big disappointments. Second, as a sick person you step away from the world of the healthy and its standards. You realize this world to which you willingly belonged is superficial and brutal—a vain and shortsighted world all the more abhorrent to a sick person. You see the illness as an opportunity to think differently and more deeply about life—and thus rise above healthy people.

Relationships may suffer as a result, but this loneliness doesn't make you sad but strong. If you weather the illness, you will have gained a new attitude to life and figured out which friends and acquaintances you can rely on, and which ones you value. Now, if someone trots out the line, "as long as you've got your health," you know that's how the healthy speak.

19.

That's Enough

I was once asked, "If you became bedridden with no hope of getting better, what would you do?" I was in my early seventies, and I think maybe the questioner expected me to say I might consider suicide, or indicate I wasn't against euthanasia. Not that I'd be indifferent to being frail and totally dependent on the help of others, but I'm not the kind of person who goes through all the eventualities in their mind and then takes every imaginable precaution. For this reason alone, the thought of suicide is foreign to me. Still, though, I found myself evading the question. I explained that I'd find it difficult to have to be fed, that I hoped to preserve my independence until the end. I talked about visiting an exhibition with a huge array of rehabilitation aids, all designed to make the everyday life of the old and sick easier. Even while I was speaking, I realized that was only half the truth.

You're beating around the bush, I said to myself. So I added, "But if I were in pain and no longer independent, would I worry about being a burden to someone else? I've been looking after other people my entire life. It would only be fair if others took care of me when I needed it. If it does come to that, I will trust in the solidarity of the generations like everyone else."

I would be all right. My confreres would take care of me. But does that make it any easier? Actually, yes, probably. But I'd still have to get used to it. It's probably the huge blow to our pride when we lose our independence that we fear most. I too will have to learn to accept help.

What doesn't scare me, though, is the thought of death. I've long since reconciled myself to the fact that at some point it will be over. And I confess I find nothing more ridiculous than the widespread tendency to smell danger everywhere. Before a trip to Rio de Janeiro, one of my colleagues who suffers from a terrible fear of flying anxiously asked me, "What if we crash?"

I gave an honest reply: "Then we'll fall out of the sky, and it's all over for us. So what?"

A philosophical answer would have been different. It would have said something about death being meaningful because it's the only thing that makes life important—that the prospect of a limited lifetime with time pressure gives us a sense of urgency and substantially increases our vitality.

To put it another way, if our life was infinite, we could put things off endlessly. Nothing would be important (except eating, drinking, and sleeping), everything would happen of its own accord, and everything could be drawn out or redone. We would live at some time or other, but not in the present. As mortals we have no time to waste, so you could say that every lifetime achievement is due to the finite nature of life.

A scientific answer would also have been different—and would have been equally in favor of death. It might argue, for example, that every individual has to pass away so that life as a whole can continue. Death makes room for new life, which picks up from the previous generation with fresh energy. Anyway, the earth already can't cope with all of us human beings—seven billion world citizens will sooner or later cause this planet to collapse. With just our current longevity, we're threatening the existence of humankind: in the future, we'll need to split between two earths if this one can have any chance to recover from the overexploitation we practice.

But however indisputable, would the fact that death is proved effective in the course of evolution reassure my colleague plagued by fear of flying? Would the fact that his mortality stimulates his productivity console him? No. I certainly wouldn't be reassured by such arguments. What makes sense to the intellect often carries no weight with the spirit. The only thing that has helped me is the experience I've had with people who were dying.

———

I have attended many confreres as they passed away. Not that this is something I have ever gotten used to. The most radical change in the world is the moment when, from one second to the next, a person ceases to be. You hold his hand, and suddenly you realize it's the hand of a dead person. With this, everything is different. Our paths have separated definitively, and another crack has run through the living world.

At such moments death is perhaps more incomprehensible than ever, but nevertheless one thing you learn over time is that it means something different to the dying person than to the person who witnesses the death. Because what seems to the living to be abrupt is for the dying a more gentle process. This at least is how it has been in those cases where I have been present. All of my confreres died reconciled, and the transition was always peaceful.

Sometimes someone was already halfway out of this world when I reached his deathbed. This is how it was with Father Callistus, who for many years had been responsible for our cowshed. That day I had an accident that totaled the car, and I got back to St. Ottilien around midnight. I wanted to fill out the damage report for the insurance company then because I was going to be busy the next morning when, at one o'clock in the morning, the porter called me. "Are you still awake? Confrere Callistus is dying. Somebody from the hospital at Landsberg has just called me."

Thank goodness there was a roadworthy car available. So off I drove again; I went to Landsberg and found Confrere Callistus where they had put him to die. He could no longer summon up the strength to speak, but I realized he recognized me from my pectoral cross. While I prayed the Sorrowful Mysteries of the Rosary, nurses repeatedly came into the room to kneel beside his bed and pray silently with me.

They didn't know Confrere Callistus, and probably, with their professional relationship to death, they would otherwise hardly have taken any notice of him. But for them, apparently my prayers had given him special value as a human being. Their participation will have done Father Callistus good, and it also helped me to fight my sleepiness. From time to time, I interrupted the Rosary with a sigh and thought, *Lord, take him; I can't go on much longer.*

And then the end came. Just as I reached the words "who died for us on the cross," Callistus ended his adventurous life—not lonely and alone, but in good company, and sometimes, that's all that counts.

In many cases, the confreres I attend are conscious, so I can witness how they arrive at a conscious acceptance of death. This acceptance is based without exception on the admission that they stand empty-handed on the threshold to the other world. In one way or another, everyone says in the last hours: "I don't have any achievement or merit with which I can stand before the Lord. I see only my shortcomings and weaknesses, but I rely on God's mercy."

Sometimes this reconciliation takes a while, when a confrere doesn't want to appear so totally naked before his Creator. But eventually everyone manages to accept the fact that "I have nothing, nothing to offer that would be of value in the eyes of the Eternal. I can only hope for his mercy." These have been valuable and sometimes also surprising experiences for me. Take, for example, the way our Father Marianus died.

He came as a priest from Berlin and had stood out all his life as demanding, difficult to please, and rarely at peace with himself and the world; he was a difficult character. Toward the end of his life, when he was already in the infirmary, he had me called to him. I went and prepared myself to hear a complaint, but this time I was wrong regarding Father Marianus.

"Father Archabbot," he said, "please don't let me be admitted to hospital. I've broken my hip, and the doctor absolutely wants me to go to hospital. But you know, I have osteoporosis, and if the hip heals tomorrow, the day after tomorrow something else will break. Please let me die in the midst of our confreres."

I insisted he remain with us as he wanted, and what a surprise—as ill-humored and almost intolerable as Father Marianus had been, he of all people faced his end fully prepared. He accepted his departure from this world like someone who says, "In two or three days I'm going on a journey, I should slowly start thinking about packing." It was certainly strange. He faced death with an acceptance he'd so often refused in life.

I was touched. After all, who can be sure of himself? At the end of life, everyone is confronted with a new task. Throughout our lives, we are eager to remain, and now we suddenly must agree to our departure. For a seriously ill person who's lost his courage to face life, that might be easy. He doesn't rebel against it any more; he gives in, exhausted and relieved, and lets himself be drawn away. But to deliberately say, "That's sufficient, that's enough," has nothing to do with resignation. To get to this state, we have to redirect our will to live in another direction. Now we look ahead and take the promise literally that the end of life's journey doesn't mean everything's over. Even in a monastery, this isn't always easy. One evening while playing cards with Father Alkuin, Prior Paul alluded to this in his ironical way.

Father Alkuin, a tall, lean figure with snow-white hair, was one of the revered missionaries at St. Ottilien. He'd been in Tanzania for over fifty years and after his return had undertaken to translate the New Testament into Swahili. Father Alkuin was making good progress, but, still, it was taking a long time. Sitting opposite him, Prior Paul looked up from his cards and made the unforgettable remark, "I know why you can't finish it. You're afraid of the last three words." The writer of Revelation pleads for the return of Jesus: "Come, Jesus Christ!"

Perhaps Prior Paul had hit the nail on the head. When the time came, it really didn't seem easy for Father Alkuin to take his leave. When I entered his hospital room two days before his death, he said with relief in his voice, "Father Archabbot, now I've made it. Now I'm ready to die. I've said yes."

With Prior Paul's remark in mind, I asked about his translation— it was my last chance. "And, Father Alkuin, did you add the last three words?"

He grinned. "Yes, yes. There was time for that too."

In the end, Prior Paul wasn't right after all.

Anyway, they all died reconciled to their situation.

And when we carried the deceased to the grave, I said to myself, *One day this is going to be you. Then the confreres will follow your coffin, just as many times you have followed one of them.* On the way out to the cemetery, the Angelorum chorus will also resound on that day, a beautiful, touching melody with a text that begins, "May the choir of the angels accompany you to heaven and take you"—and so in death, anchored in the community of the confreres as I was in life, my journey will cease.

> Like a weaver I have rolled up my life;
>> he cuts me off from the loom;
> from day to night you bring me to an end.

So says the prophet Isaiah (38:12). I am prepared for it.

I even know the place where I will come to lie at St. Ottilien. Not in the crypt, the traditional resting place of the abbots; it's too venerable for me down there. I prefer to be buried where all the others lie, in our monastery cemetery among my confreres. Close the cover of my coffin, let me down into the earth, and let me molder in peace: that's my only wish. I won't specify anything else for after my death. I know what's been done with dead abbots in the course of history. I don't want to fall into the hand of the Gunther von Hagenses of this world, who might prepare and exhibit me, skinned but with the pectoral cross around my neck.

———•◆•———

Meanwhile arrangements for my death have already been made at St. Ottilien. Under the big cemetery cross, four graves for abbots have been prepared. The first is already occupied, and one of three others awaits me. I do, however, attach importance to the solemn burial of my body according to the old rite, with the old chants. The modern practice of soundless disappearance without a trace—just put the urn in its niche or scatter the ashes and that's that—is not my way. For me it's a sign of respect to the dead person to bury his body in a manner that befits his dignity.

In a cemetery, the dead also remain a part of the human race; here the living have a place of remembrance; here a feeling of closeness with the previous generations can be established. And just as a cemetery reveals the past through the graves, it also gives us a glimpse of the future; here the living can move out of the confines of the present into a time period that stretches away into the distance. What other place can you say that of?

But I don't want to be misunderstood: burial is not a Christian commandment. Whether cremation or a grave in the ground is your final resting place is a purely practical question—even monks have been cremated, and in some cemeteries only urns are accepted for lack of space.

Although, it's true that when Freemasons began cremating their dead in the nineteenth century as an atheistic demonstration against the resurrection of the body, the Church reacted with outrage. It took a while for the Church to understand that resurrection can't depend on the condition of the dead person. What would happen in that case to all those who were burned or torn to pieces in war or other disasters? With Vatican II, the attitude of the Church toward cremation of the dead changed. This practice is no longer considered disrespectful to the faith; for Christians, it's as acceptable as classic burial.

From the beginning, it would have been better to listen to the apostle Paul, who uses the image of the seed to talk about death and resurrection. As the seed placed into the soil gives no indication of the plant that will emerge from it, so there will be an unpredictable transformation when the dead human body is resurrected. The resurrection of the body is a divine secret, and we can work neither toward nor against it.

⟶◆◆⟵

Sometimes, personal experiences help with navigating this issue more than theological debate. Here I'll never forget the celebration some years ago to mark the nine-hundredth anniversary of the death of our patron Anselm of Canterbury.

For the final concert in our church, we had invited an orchestra from the Italian city of L'Aquila. When planning the concert, we'd thought only of the glorious music of Pergolesi and Vivaldi, and then came the earthquake that destroyed L'Aquila. The musicians had survived, but only because they'd been performing in another city the night of the catastrophe. Many had lost their homes, and some were mourning family members killed when their houses collapsed. They themselves were living in a tent village or with friends or relatives.

These musicians had every reason to cancel the concert. Everyone would have understood if they'd not touched their instruments after this incident, if they'd felt unable to play for a time. But they came. Music, they said, had become their language of hope, and that evening a power poured out of their instruments that I wouldn't have thought possible.

Every chord was the expression of a common confidence, and the audience left feeling that life will triumph over death just as joy had triumphed over sorrow during that hour. The suffering of these musicians moved us deeply; we felt all the more that their music was a message of their faith, and that message was that the forces of destruction will not prevail.

It was as if we'd all been witnesses of the resurrection.

20.

Little Wand'rer, Soul of Mine

The resurrection of the dead isn't talked about much these days. Nor is eternal life. And it's been a long time since I've heard that wild cry of triumph unleashed by the apostle Paul in the First Letter to the Corinthians:

> O death, where is your victory?
> O death, where is your sting? (1 Cor. 15:55 ESV)

But this is also an incredible thing to say. Here is somebody daring to ridicule death with the almost insane joy of someone who sees a tyrant overthrown. What exuberant joy!

Today talking about eternal life is more likely to make you unpopular. Some people are positively indignant: *Kid's stuff! Cheap consolation!* So they'd rather have no life goal than eternal bliss? Even among theologians now, you can disgrace yourself if you deny the omnipotence of death.

"Do you *really* believe in heaven?" someone asked me.

"Yes," I replied. "I believe in heaven." He smiled pityingly as if it wasn't possible to have a serious conversation with someone like me.

But is there a more beautiful hope than that for life after death? Wouldn't this fulfill our greatest longing? Haven't all human beings, regardless of culture, believed from time immemorial in a hereafter? The items buried in every Stone Age grave we discover prove that the occupant was convinced he or she was beginning a journey to another, better existence. And of course we Christians have always said farewell to our dead in the hope of meeting again. But now all of a sudden this is declared to be ridiculous. Nothing continues. With death everything is over.

Have we become wiser?

I don't know how anyone can be so sure about this. But I do know that if we think death brings down the curtain definitively, we condemn ourselves to a meaningless life. Because then our life is going nowhere. So why not consider the second possibility: eternal life instead of an eternal void? Lowered curtains can be raised again. Perhaps we start thinking very differently about this, the closer we are to death?

I, at least, am not convinced by the arguments against eternal life; they satisfy neither my reason nor my feelings. Why should I exchange one belief for another? No one knows what comes afterward. "For we walk by faith, not by sight" (2 Cor. 5:7), says the apostle Paul, but that applies right through life. We've never known whether our hopes will be fulfilled, and this uncertainty has never bothered us; it's never prevented us from hoping for all sorts of things throughout our lives.

Human beings consist of hope, as if it were the stuff of which we are made. Why should we now suddenly be overcome by an unprecedented hopelessness in the face of death? Whoever reproaches Christians for consoling themselves with an illusion is also clinging to an illusion, and it's an extremely sad one.

Human beings after all have not only a bodily but also a spiritual dimension, the soul, which can't be harmed by time and is the source of our irrepressible appetite for life. All the faiths of the human race so far believe that this soul lives on when the body dies and decays. The Old Testament alludes to this in beautifully poetic words when it speaks of the breath of God that returns to God after death; today we would talk instead about energy that also remains when forms disappear.

Religions differ about the destiny of the soul once separated from the body—it wanders and enters a new body; it's banished forever to an underworld; it rises to the light and participates in the glory of God—there are many different possibilities, but extinction isn't one of them. Even when its survival isn't associated with any hope of a better life, as with the ancient Romans and Greeks, the soul isn't extinguished.

What is this universal belief based on? Not on experience, at any rate. On an intuition common to all? Maybe, I don't know. But because belief in the immortality of the soul is part of the human conceptual world, I'd like to follow up on this and go into more detail about the two interpretations of the afterlife that suggest themselves to someone living in Rome: that of pagan antiquity (from the Aventine we overlook the Circus Maximus with the colossal ruins of the Palatine behind it), and that of Christianity.

———

Roman and Greek thinking about the hereafter seems very strange indeed to us today. The soul was immortal for them, but this was their misfortune. The philosophically educated, art-loving emperor Hadrian summarized this dilemma on his deathbed in these few heartbreakingly beautiful lines:

> Little wand'rer, soul of mine,
> That dost within the body stay,
> Now thy dwelling-place is gone,

Whither wilt thou go away,
Pale, defenceless, stiff and chill?
hush'd is thy wonted voice and still.
(Translation by Byron)

I can read these five lines again and again, and they always move me. In the few seconds it takes to read them, we learn so much about the person Hadrian and the thinking of his time. Here we're obviously witnessing a farewell scene and listening to a soliloquy—a very intimate moment—and you almost want to take a discreet step back, but then you hesitate and ask yourself, *Who's actually speaking? Who's actually bidding such a melancholy, resigned farewell—and to whom?* And suddenly you realize that the emperor is bidding farewell to himself. Not to the world as we might have expected, but to himself.

He's still what he's been his entire life, a complete human being, a unit consisting of body and soul, but now dissolution is imminent, the dissolution of his personality. And then it's not the world he'll miss; it's not his body he's mourning—it's his soul that has loved this world and is certainly not weary of it, because the emperor is just sixty-two when he dies. Although the body is mentioned, it's almost in passing and without regret, but on his soul Hadrian lovingly plants a farewell kiss before it separates from his body and both go their own way in death.

The tenderness of this gesture can't conceal the bitterness of the moment, however, because, what awaits his soul? A dismal realm of shades where it faces the endless monotony of a disembodied existence. So according to the thinking of antiquity, immortality is fatal for the soul. Separated from the body, it's homeless and unsheltered and condemned to imprisonment in the realm of death until the end of time.

All joy, Hadrian tells us, is joy in life and therefore tied up with the unity of body and soul. In this light, this apparently serene death poem is both a glowing declaration of love for life—this is probably also why it's so touching and beautiful—and a cry of pain in the face of complete hopelessness.

The prospect is not comforting. The body decays, the soul is deserted—and that's it. In antiquity, death is connected with nothing but loss and renunciation; all you can do is resign gracefully with wistful fatalism, as Hadrian does. But evidently, this graceful attitude toward death was not widespread.

Seneca reports scenes of desperation in the last days and hours of his contemporaries: "But see how these same people clasp the knees of physicians if they fall ill and the danger of death draws nearer, see how ready they are, if threatened with capital punishment, to spend all their possessions in order to live."

You can feel the existential distress, unmitigated by hope, which probably comes closer to the reality for most Romans of that time. In pagan antiquity we find both unwavering, stoical acceptance of death and naked fear of dying. What we do not find is confident serenity, the positively joyful consent with which many Christians met their death at that time—and with which they often still accept death today.

----◆----

O death, where is your sting? O death, where is your victory? The exuberance of the apostle Paul must have seemed strange to the Romans. Christians imagined something better than earthly existence, and this would have been positively unnerving to their pagan contemporaries. This Christian belief didn't come out of the blue, though. For them, the crucified and risen Christ was the guarantor of eternal life, and they believed the witnesses.

Was it out of naïveté, as their pagan contemporaries suspected? If you look closely at the reports in the Gospels, you'll find that they don't nourish a naïve belief in miracles at all. Instead, the events tax the mind and imagination to the utmost, and the Evangelists have trouble finding words for them. They relate what happened after the discovery of the empty grave with a storm of emotions.

Every encounter of the disciples, both women and men, with the Risen Lord unleashes a mixture of the most contradictory sentiments— fear, horror, shock, consternation, doubt, joy, exultation—and often doubt and fear predominate. Because there's a problem with the Risen Lord: he's unrecognizable. At least visibly. He can't be identified from his appearance, stature, and face.

In his new form of existence, Jesus doesn't even look familiar to those closest to him—his appearance says nothing to them at first glance. This is the case with Mary Magdalene, with the Emmaus disciples, with Thomas, and even with Peter and John; none of them associates Jesus with his external appearance. In the accounts it says repeatedly that *they did not recognize him.*

Even the stigmata, the marks of the Crucifixion, don't make things clear. This is not the Jesus they are familiar with, it's not the body they know, so no wonder they don't associate the person before them with him. Every appearance of the Risen Lord gives rise to misunderstanding, guesswork, speculation, aggravation, and even oppression—the people who see him can no longer believe their eyes.

It's not that the Risen Lord is an anonymous stranger—he does not seem to have visible personal or individual characteristics. He no longer belongs to the visible world, even though he's perfectly visible. Other distinguishing characteristics are required. It's at the sound of his voice, by the way he speaks, or from certain gestures or habits that he's suddenly recognized, from one incident to the next.

In the encounter with Mary Magdalene, Jesus has to say her name for her to recognize him. The Emmaus disciples only realize by the way he breaks bread who is before them. These nonbodily characteristics connect the Risen Jesus to the earthly Jesus. It's still him, but in a strange way he's both familiar and unfamiliar.

But the transformation goes much further: while the Risen Lord has a body, this body has extraordinary features, as if it were made of another substance. It is not subject to the conditions of space and time or the limitations of a natural body. He appears when and where he wants, unhindered by walls and distances, and he disappears in the same way—all of a sudden.

The accounts of these events rule out the two possible explanations for his unexpected return from the grave: that it's the ghost of a dead person, or that Jesus miraculously survived his crucifixion.

Both, incidentally, would be banal and not worth talking about. A dead person who says, "Here I am again," is at best unearthly; someone who survives a crucifixion, at most a medical curiosity. No, what the disciples encounter here is neither an earthly body nor a ghost, and the Evangelists make every effort to make sure there's no confusion. In John and Luke, the Risen Lord even eats food as ultimate proof that this is no ghost, no phantom from the realm of the dead, as the disciples apparently suspect.

But what is he then? What kind of body, what kind of human being, are we dealing with here? Even more remarkable, those who encounter Jesus cannot or may not touch this body. Either the Risen Jesus won't let himself be touched, or the people he meets shy away from the possibility.

"Do not hold on to me" (John 20:17), he says to Mary Magdalene when she throws herself at his feet.

"Stay with us" (Lk. 24:29), urge the Emmaus disciples, but shortly afterward the body of Jesus dissolves into thin air, as it were.

And although the Risen Lord has invited him to do so, Thomas, the doubting disciple, hesitates to put his finger into the wounds on Jesus's body (John 20:24–28).

Apparently this is a bodily presence that belongs to a different reality.

Taken as a whole, we see that the resurrection of Jesus doesn't take the form of a triumphant return. It disturbs all those involved, and the way it's told by the Evangelists, it has a similar effect on the reader: disciples who don't erupt with joy at the sight of the Risen Lord; a Christ who has great difficulties convincing his old companions of his identity. This is, at any rate, not a light religious diet for gullible and simple souls. But it's precisely because it is a mysterious, confusing story that I feel it contains important clues from the Risen Lord to guide our thinking about eternal life.

I think that in these reports we're witnessing a real but totally different form of existence. An existence in a new, higher dimension, a kind of timeless presence.

Horror, fear, shock, the entire storm of feelings that engulfs those involved is triggered by an occurrence never before experienced: the penetration of the divine or eternal reality into everyday reality. This other reality leaves the witnesses helpless and speechless. They can't talk about it directly, but must talk about it—these experiences are real. The Evangelists thus face the impossible task of putting what is beyond expression into words. They must translate something that transcends all our concepts into language, no matter how inadequate. And while searching for words and pictures, they unavoidably get enmeshed in contradictions, and inevitably don't go far enough. However, this process renders them not less credible but more so—they manage to describe the unimaginable, if perhaps a little clumsily.

For me, the Resurrection reveals the mystery of the divine reality without our being able to understand or define it; nevertheless, something about that other reality can be learned from the experiences with the Risen Lord if faith comes to the aid of the overextended mind. We only need to look at the letters of the apostle Paul, in the places where he talks about the resurrection of the dead and eternal life, approximately twenty years after the Resurrection.

He, too, wisely contents himself with allusions. He can't be blamed for what the painters of subsequent ages made of this, a Day of Judgment with half-decayed bodies wriggling out of the soil into the daylight like worms. In the fifteenth chapter of the First Letter to the Corinthians, where Paul describes the resurrection of the dead in detail, he speaks only of a transformation at the moment of resurrection and a new, imperishable body.

With the image of the Risen Lord in mind, we can at least get an idea of this transformation, this new body. Moreover we can be certain our personality will be preserved in this transformed state. We won't disappear into the anonymous realm of disembodied souls. The body is part of our individuality, and even if it has nothing in common with our former earthly body, we'll experience eternity as individuals. That's one side of it.

The other side is eternity. Abbot Hugo, of St. Boniface in Munich, once said, "Heaven can wait, it's going to be beautiful for all eternity." At the time, his words were greeted with approving smiles, but unfortunately they were based on a fallacy. There's nothing in the Scriptures to suggest we should think of eternity as an endless extension of our present life, as if eternal life were a never-ending life. Something quite different is meant: not an indefinite extension of time, but the suspension of time—a life with God that takes place purely in the present, life in a totally different dimension.

Augustine chooses the Latin expression *nunc stans*, which could be translated as "immortal, everlasting moment." What will that be like? I have no idea; we'll see. But at least if we are aware of this difference, we won't be fooled by the banal images of heaven as a playground of harp-playing, white-robed souls.

I fear these false images derived from antiquity and Greek mythology have been fixed in our minds. We paint eternity as a cheerful counterpart of the realm of shades where we'll continue in the same manner as on earth, but disembodied. Of course, we can't help thinking this might be overwhelmingly boring—an uneventful afterlife isn't tempting, however pleasant it's made to seem. But unfortunately, such portrayals seem to have influenced our picture of eternity more strongly than the much more subtle indications of the New Testament.

Both painters and poets have contributed to this. I think of Dante, who goes through the circles of heaven and hell in his *Divine Comedy* as if there this life is duplicated in the life beyond and the natural laws of space and time remain valid in eternity. Very little of the mystery of the Scriptures remains. With his powerful words, Dante created images that contradict the Christian faith—and probably did him considerable damage.

It is simply beyond our powers of imagination. I remember the famous New Testament scholar Otto Kuss expressing the same opinion in his lectures. With their efforts to make the invisible visible, he said, artists have done a lot of damage to belief, because in their work the eternal assumes a form so strongly influenced by their eras and cultures that it is no longer compatible with the divine mystery.

So take up the Bible occasionally and compare what you think you believe with the testimony of the Holy Scripture. Otherwise you'll end up talking about art when you think you're talking about religion.

———

A personal word at the end of this chapter. As I get older, the resurrection of Jesus occupies me more and more. I even find that the figure of Jesus Christ has become more important for me altogether over the years. He comes closer to me, or I come closer to him. My relationship with Christ used to be different, more impersonal, perhaps more theological. Now it's as if I am getting to know Jesus again, in a new way, as if I were somehow able to exchange experiences with him. Now, toward the end of my life, something I previously knew only intellectually is touching me deeply: that he is the liberator, the redeemer. He also liberates us from external forms of piety. He turns our eyes to God and prepares us for our own resurrection. The world, with its undoubtedly fascinating richness, is put into perspective for me, and it becomes clearer and clearer that we own nothing. Everything must be given back. Everything was in a mysterious sense only a preparation for another, new existence, of which the eyewitness reports in the Gospels give us an indication.

The question of the Resurrection is anyway becoming more concrete, more urgent and ever-present. That's how it is: anyone approaching death moves toward the Risen Lord, who belongs to another reality although he is present in the world. This approach introduces a new tension into my life. I'm still clinging to this world, but at the same time I'm detaching myself from it. What is essential? What is unimportant? The old question once again requires new answers when you notice that your time's running out, and soon you'll no longer be here.

In the end, Jesus remains as the crucial figure in the life of a Christian. Why should we doubt his resurrection and eternal life, when even a declared atheist like Arthur Schopenhauer says, "When death closes our eyes, we will stand in a light of which the light of the sun is just a shadow"?

21.

Overcoming Loneliness

I've assembled the following list of sixteen strengths and benefits of old age:

Unpretentiousness
Humor
Serenity
Straightforwardness
Freedom
Patience
Wisdom
Authority
Wealth of knowledge and experience
Benevolence
Generosity
Humanitarianism
Sovereignty
Knowledge of human nature
Resoluteness
Courageousness

I've already talked about most of these privileges and achievements, and some I've dealt with in detail, but perhaps only a list like this can make us aware of the amazing wealth of resources at our disposal after sixty or seventy years of life. Of course not everyone will identify with all these characteristics or possess them all to the same degree. But even in smaller doses they form a solid foundation for contentment in old age. And if, for a change, you study the faces of old people in public, you'll find that many of them actually reflect these characteristics.

But not all of them. You will see faces marked by resentment, resignation, and bitterness too. You will meet people who regard age as a curse and bemoan their condition. Of course this may be related to an illness. But in my experience, those who have every reason to complain because they are seriously ill, who have to undergo protracted, unpleasant treatments like dialysis and radiation—they are seldom the ones who complain. It's almost always those with less threatening maladies who want to be pitied.

A much more common reason for depression in old age is feeling lonely. Nothing seems to depress the old more than the feeling that no one notices them anymore, that they're no longer respected, that they're surrounded by a world of strangers. It's estimated that in Germany there are several million people who don't exchange a personal word with anyone else for days, sometimes weeks, at a time.

How can this be? Are these people who've been forgotten by their relatives and live in nursing homes or hospitals? Are they people imprisoned in their own four walls because they're no longer mobile? Or people who have no one to talk with because they've outlived all their friends?

Sometimes, it seems to me, loneliness in old age is more of a self-inflicted situation—though I'm not saying the people concerned are at fault. Friendships and acquaintances have to be cultivated, and some people are so monopolized by their jobs that for years, decades even, they have no time to maintain their precious store of friendships. I remember a conversation with the director of a culture center, an open-minded woman who was nevertheless left without any friends after retirement.

"My ambition was to constantly provide this culture center with fresh impetus and keep it going despite a lack of funds," she said, "but it was a full-time job, which barely gave me a free minute. Inevitably, I neglected old friendships, and so one after another my friends slipped away. In the long run, even your best friend resents it if you never have time for her. But what should I have done? My involvement gave me great pleasure, and it had a purpose."

She isn't an isolated case. You may have a job you like where you constantly meet new, interesting people, but the acquaintanceships are fleeting, this work eats up all your attention, and eventually even the people closest to your heart disappointedly withdraw. This will take its toll in old age.

Normally, friendships can withstand a lot. Often, they're more resilient than family relationships; they can even survive long periods of separation, provided that separation is because of physical distance. But if you live in the same city and only show your face once in a blue moon, at some point the other person will suspect indifference, and this poisons any friendship. One of our main goals in life should be to keep firm hold of our friendships. They are the most reliable remedy against loneliness in old age.

Of course, not everyone in old age develops the delightful sense of humor I encountered in Elisabetta and her friend sitting on that bench long ago, which I described back in chapter 1. Some go in the opposite direction and become grumpy. They are bothered by one thing in one friend and annoyed by something else in another. They can't overlook offenses, and yet another old friend falls out of favor forever by saying the wrong thing. And as a result, their circle of friends disintegrates.

And in old age you have less drive; you tire more easily. You dread the energy involved in conflict. This means you're more likely to say, "What's the point?" and withdraw. In these cases, too, the loneliness is self-inflicted. I'm reminded of the following episode at St. Ottilien.

A confrere asked for exclaustration, a temporary break from monastic life, because he couldn't stand the loneliness in the monastery—no one visited him. My first response was to ask whether he visited other people.

"No," he answered.

Well, it was absurd, but I didn't want us to show any lack of care, so to the next person I met, I said, "You two get on pretty well. Go and visit him; he's complaining about loneliness."

"I sat with him yesterday evening over a bottle of wine," was the answer.

I spoke to a second person: "Can you visit him? He feels lonely."

"I went to see him a few days ago with a bottle of wine," was the reply.

So, then I did support the exclaustration of the lonely confrere, but it was because of his acute loss of reality.

You have to reach out to others. As long you can leave your home on your own or even with the help of others, you must mix with people. Life is participation; life is being part of the community, and age is no reason to stop being involved in the affairs of the world as if you had nothing to offer, as if you'd become unacceptable to younger people or even to your own age group.

Sitting offended in the corner is no remedy against loneliness. But Elisabetta and her friend, sitting contentedly in the sun in front of the house, and picking the right moment to say something—that certainly is. I know quite a few people who always wait for others to approach them; then, of course, loneliness can't be averted. Then all that really remains is the sofa and the TV.

I don't know how common this is nowadays, but when my mother was old she met her friends every week for coffee; they took turns hosting. And when she was in the hospital, there wasn't a single day when she didn't have a visitor. Right up until her death at eighty-five, loneliness was not a word in her vocabulary.

Apart from such established circles of friends, though, just leave the house and there are so many ways to make contact with others, ranging from a chat with the waiter over a cappuccino in a café to striking up a conversation with the person sitting at your table in an old folk's club run by a church or association—to book clubs, event series, and courses. Recently, for example, I heard about a crafts group for women of all ages that meets in the charming, stimulating atmosphere of a small theater. They create something with their hands and then sit together over a cup of coffee and homemade cakes. Why shouldn't new acquaintances result out of that, perhaps between members of different generations?

Of course, it may sometimes be an effort to initiate contact—maybe previous disappointments hold you back—but loneliness ought to end the moment you leave the house.

But then, it's also not quite as simple as that. If you live to a ripe old age and experience the thinning of the ranks as old friends and long-standing companions bid farewell one after the other, at some point you will in fact be left alone with your life story. You will have become a relic. It's not just that your confidants are gone; there will hardly be anyone left who shares similar experiences and memories. This threatens you with the worst form of loneliness: abandonment.

Not even celebrity seems to protect from this. The famous philosopher Hannah Arndt complained toward the end of her life that her familiar world was dissolving and nothing remained but a desert of unfamiliar faces, unfamiliar fashions, and unfamiliar ways of thinking. In other words, the old are condemned to rootlessness.

This form of loneliness is hard to escape. At some point, the way you express yourself (even your handwriting alone) will reveal that you no longer belong to the current age, and there will be more and more moments when you feel yourself positively cast out of the present. You mention a name—of a famous actor or athlete from your day—you of course assume that everyone knows him or her, but you reap only uncomprehending gazes—younger people have never heard the name; it means nothing to them.

What you say finds fewer and fewer echoes in this world, and you can't ignore the fact that you've become the past, history—that you're the last example of an extinct race. Eighty years are half an eternity, and if you're so inclined, you can see your own youth in a docudrama on TV.

This is undoubtedly discouraging, but I wonder if forfeiting your right of residence in the present when you're very old is inevitable.

———— ⬩ ————

It's different for me, of course. In the order I'm already spoiled because we're constantly among our confreres and meet at least at meals and the Liturgy of the Hours. I sometimes find the turmoil too much. Over the years, my need for quiet has become stronger; I'm increasingly bothered by noise, and I have a growing wish to be left alone for a time, to be able to come to myself and focus on myself.

It's not that I'm withdrawing; it's rather that so much accumulates in my head that I need a few hours in between to deal with it. Afterward, however, everything can go on as before, and I try to have at least a few minutes for everyone. When the ladies at Fiumicino airport check-in beckon me and say, "Come right over here," of course I ask how they are!

I can't get by without a regular injection of human warmth, and I'd find it terrible to plow a lonely furrow.

What the family is for the other people, the order is for me. Here you experience a natural cohesion that stands the test in personal crises and miraculously functions across the generations. On the other hand, the most important anchor and life preserver in a family is the spouse or life partner. One of the most beautiful images to me is that of an old couple sitting quietly side by side in the sun with closed eyes and joined hands—a true picture of earthly happiness.

But you can rely on the family less and less. Separation and divorce have become the norm, and loneliness for some begins in the fifth or sixth decade of life—at some point, discouraged, you give up searching for a new partner and remain alone. There's always been a lot of irreconcilability in families. I repeatedly hear of children who've turned away from father, mother, or both. And families are often scattered, with only loose contact between children and elderly parents.

So often, family and marriage don't provide the security that was once their greatest strength. Neighbors can compensate to some extent. In your building or on your road, you can get to know people, and then it depends on what you make of it. Will it go beyond neutral conversations on the stairs to becoming friends with one another and sometimes inviting the young couple over for dinner?

Closeness like this can happen of its own accord—these may not be friends for life, but you should no more despise good acquaintances than you should the little chats "over the garden fence" or a cup of coffee or glass of wine. And when you need someone, someone will be there. The best place for opportunities for casual contact to arise is in the neighborhood. You just have to pluck up courage. But on no account say to yourself, "You can't expect that of me; I'm not putting myself through that anymore," and barricade yourself in your four walls.

Nothing can replace true friends, though. Only friendship generates the life-giving feeling of being at home in this world. You need somebody to indulge in shared memories with, somebody you can say one word to and you both laugh, somebody you can unburden your heart to and talk openly about anything. But if you want friends, you have to do something about it. You can't neglect friendship because of family and career; it will only be more difficult later, simply because friendship is built on shared experiences, and at seventy, most people aren't game for any new ones.

It's not enough to just hold on for decades to friends from your own generation. The best thing is to have friendships with people of different generations, with significantly older and significantly younger ones. This doesn't just widen your horizons with a steady flow of new perspectives; it also makes you better prepared for your own old age. Because the old teach you how to grow old and die, and the young are there when it's your turn. A person who makes friends in other age groups will very soon realize that the gap in years makes no difference to the relationship.

＊

As I've said, friendship is a lifelong project, and at some point, you can't catch up. Lapsed friendships can only rarely be revived, and new ones need time to grow. There are ways of compensating somewhat for the absence of friends in old age, though. In my opinion, the easiest is to join an amateur choir. They are like psychosocial power stations— whoever joins is accepted into a veritable extended family, and finds that singing together overcomes barriers, internal and external.

This is in the nature of music. I believe that singing in a choir is life-giving. Although old people are withdrawing from life, music can restore them to it again. When you study a composition, you are involved body and soul in the creative process. You feel with all your senses how a work is maturing inside you and gradually coming to full bloom, and this gives you a feeling of joy comparable with the joy of younger days. Then on the day of the concert, as one of many, you produce something vibrant and beautiful for an audience that is infected with your own joy.

All this is exciting and liberating, and it connects you to other people. During rehearsals, together you experience all that music does: you feel strong emotions, you expose yourself to dramatic sentiments—and you feel close to one another in a unique way. Music always creates community; it always shows us that more connects us than divides us. So acquaintances and friendships can arise easily through singing together.

Choir community includes all generations and makes it easier than elsewhere to come into contact with people of all ages. Older members will be particularly grateful for this. I have seen friendships grow between young singers and members over eighty.

Music enlivens. It promotes togetherness. And it can help mitigate the big problem of age: loneliness.

Of course the best thing would be to remain involved in friendships and family relationships through to the end. It certainly makes it easier to endure all the unpleasant aspects of old age. But I'm certain that loneliness is in no way an inevitable fate. We just have to show the world we're still here.

22.

On the Fading of the World

In addition to his well-known novels, short stories, and ballads, Theodor Fontane also wrote poems. They are the melancholy late works of a man undergoing an orderly process of withdrawal, who can only silently shake his head over the major and minor dramas of life. This is my favorite poem of his:

> Early today, having slept the whole night,
> I rose into the morning light.
> Breakfast was ready and waiting for me,
> The roll toasted fresh, and hot was the coffee,
> I sat to read the paper then
> (Promotions were being made again).
> I stepped to the window and looked outside,
> The city was starting to get into stride,
> (At the butcher's) an apron hung over a stool
> Little girls were out walking to school—
> Everything friendly, everything gay
> But if I had just stayed in bed the whole day,

> Pretending to be unaware of all this,
> Would there be something I'd possibly miss?

Here somebody's politely saying farewell to a world that no longer interests him. Even the poem doesn't seem to mean much to him; it sounds brittle and almost carelessly composed, as if it had been written by a tired hand. He has nothing earth-shattering to say, as he did earlier in his great ballads; he just gives us a little soliloquy in the late evening of life, a brief farewell letter to the world that is fading before his eyes.

No, no regrets, no complaints. It's not unbearable, this world—the coffee comes hot out of the pot; the roll is just right, crispy, and still warm; the newspaper has nothing more exciting in it than the promotions of a few officers; and on the street everything looks reassuringly ordinary. Everything's on an even keel. But he can no longer enjoy these little things of life that he'd only really learned to appreciate a few years previously.

Now, at the end of his seventies, he has entered a new phase of life, and a good-natured indifference has taken possession of him: Everything's pretty, everything's nice, but if you slept on, if you perhaps never got out of bed, what would you miss? Nothing, he says. And the thought doesn't frighten him at all. The old Fontane has already put one foot out of this world and notes with relief that it's become entirely dispensable. Something you'd never have thought possible.

The desire to let go, the desire to say goodbye—I'm discovering signs of that in myself as well. When I gaze around my study, I conclude that I could part from most of what's there without a pang. The many souvenirs from Africa, Asia, and South America; all the statues and figures on the shelves: What did I want them for? Why was I so keen to have them? I've lost my passion for collecting, and the beloved souvenirs have become dust collectors sitting around like any other thing, and I no longer feel proud of owning them when I look at them.

And the contents of my wardrobe? I don't need most of what's in there. I'd really like to clear it out—two pairs of pants and two jackets ought to be enough. With things that connect me to the past, I've thrown away some; others I've given a grace period for reverential reasons. But I've decided the current contents will serve me until the end of my life. Nothing new will be added.

In any case, I understand Pope Francis's message to reduce all expenditure and requirements to the essential much better today than I used to. Declutter radically. Most things are dispensable—and it is more accurate to say they are distracting and encumbering—a self-made prison, a millstone round your neck, nothing but an obstacle on the road ahead of you. Get rid of them in order to be free. A desire for freedom is occupying an increasingly important place in my life.

Some things have a practical value. I need a car, for example, to be able to move around in Rome and Italy, mainly from Sant'Anselmo to the Fiumicino airport and back, and I still enjoy driving—I don't find myself getting more anxious. (Though mostly I'm driven by a volunteer so I can keep working.) I still like to get behind the steering wheel; I still like the feeling of acceleration when I put my foot on the pedal.

But my new ascetic outlook makes its appearance again in the way I experience sensual pleasure: my perception has sharpened. I don't need as much anymore, but I enjoy the little I have more intensively.

Here I'm also developing a feel for the subtler things of life: the aromatic air of the Mediterranean summer, for example; a bouquet of flowers with which someone has decorated my guest room; the way a sister almost lovingly strokes the water jug as she carefully sets it down on the table in front of me—testimonies of beauty, goodness, and kindness that would perhaps previously have gone unnoticed. I'm practicing for the time when all the excitement is over.

Even my meals are more modest, as I've already mentioned; I choose more carefully, limit myself, hold back, and discover that moderation promotes enjoyment. This is an old piece of wisdom; even Epicurus understood the correlation between self-discipline and sensual pleasure.

On this subject Robert Spaemann, a modern philosopher, said, "Anyone who can really enjoy what reality has to offer, doesn't need much of it." And he adds, "Whoever manages with little, is more certain of rarely missing anything." So, at the least, my new way will mean I will be fine getting smaller doses of pleasures for whatever reasons.

In addition to this deliberate moderation, old age is characterized by a new form of humility. As a monk you've learned neither to claim services nor to place value on them. In Sant'Anselmo, for example, people take turns serving at table during meals, everyone distributes the meals, even our professors, and I occasionally help out too. If a button comes off my jacket minutes before departure for the airport, as happened again recently, then once I'm on the plane I sew it back on myself, getting surprised looks from the flight attendant.

Self-sufficiency and independence are requirements of the monastic life, and for this reason I find it difficult to surrender my suitcase to a confrere who can't stand by and watch his abbot primate struggle. I see it as an exercise in humility to let myself be helped in such situations—everyone's familiar with this who has reached a certain age and is offered a seat in a crowded train by a younger person for the first time. This too is an exercise in humility: to swallow one's displeasure at this cheeky cub, this hateful brat, to feign gratitude and grudgingly take the proffered seat. Let's be honest, it's nice to have a seat and take the weight off your feet. Even I don't need to be constantly on the move.

I'm not giving away any secrets when I say that being a hermit wouldn't have been the right thing for me, but still, I can manage to stay at home for three or four days at a time—sometimes there's an accumulation of meetings here at Sant'Anselmo, and sometimes I might lock myself in my study to write sermons or lectures (which in the end will involve prolonged standing). I like taking such breaks from the whirl of appointments. Anyway, I like to take particular care and time with the text for my speeches, because I say to myself, *Every lecture is a wonderful opportunity to introduce Christian thought outside the Church and in a wide variety of contexts—perhaps something will stick in the minds of the businesspeople, politicians, young managers, and bankers in your audience.*

I can only sow—the sower has no influence on the kind of soil, fertile or infertile, on which the seeds fall, as Jesus makes clear in his famous parable. Nevertheless, of course, you sow in the hope that the seed will sprout and bear good fruit. So I don't want to offer a run-of-the-mill speech. And sometimes, at the last minute, I'm dissatisfied with what I've written, and I tear it up when I'm already on the plane to the venue and prepare a new one at lightning speed (which is possible only because I don't write out every word of my speeches).

———

I've already gathered momentum again. Yes, it's true, despite some slight tendencies toward gradual withdrawal, I'm a very long way from that melancholy indifference with which Theodor Fontane distances himself from life.

But for me, too, the day will come in the not too distant future, when it'll be, *Arrivederci, Sant'Anselmo, arrivederci Roma.* And then? What will be next? Will I fall into the famous black hole? Will I fulfill long-postponed wishes? Will I abandon myself to the sweet idleness that was never granted to me in, of all places, the city of *dolce far niente*?

I'm increasingly being asked such questions. I have a typical Roman answer, *Vediamo*. We'll see. Because I don't know what's going to happen. I haven't wasted any thought on an exit strategy. As is my wont, I will simply let the day of my retirement and all the following days come, but I suspect the world won't fade for me so quickly. My enthusiastic participation in the life and fate of others suggests otherwise, and I suspect this will triumph.

Only one thing is clear regarding my future: I'll turn my back on Rome and live again at St. Ottilien—the monastery not far from Ammersee that I entered as a twenty-year-old in 1961. That's my monastic base; that's where I'm at home. Not that I've had enough of this terrific, chaotic, strenuous, and lovable Rome—by no means—but I'll also be happy to go back to that abbey where I served as archabbot for the extraordinarily long time of twenty-three years.

I'm looking forward to being among my confreres again—also considering that when I was archabbot, I admitted not only my direct successor but also his successor, the present Archabbot Wolfgang, into the novitiate. No, St. Ottilien did not become unfamiliar to me during my absence, and it is there, not Rome, where I will find what is more precious the older I get: the intimate, familiar atmosphere that St. Benedict envisioned as ideal when he founded his first monastery.

My only fear is that even there, I won't be seen watching the hustle and bustle outside my window with disinterested pleasure as did Fontane, in his fine poem, looking out on Berlin.

For the simple reason that I probably won't have time.

But until then, I continue to work in Rome and hope to fulfill my responsibilities well—in other words, remain in good health so I can complete my work. Of course, I know the completion of my projects is not in my hands. Like any other mortal, I'll leave only fragments behind.

But that doesn't bother me. I am not irreplaceable; I'm even completely dispensable. Others will continue my work.

Early on, I relinquished the illusion of total responsibility, and since then I have never interfered in everything, never felt responsible for all the details. It helps if you tell yourself, *Others also have a mind and are no stupider than you.* When I was called to Rome, I told my successor at St. Ottilien, "I won't interfere. I'm giving you a free hand. If necessary slaughter my holy cows. I won't protest; I'll see it rather as a sign of vitality."

And he has slaughtered some of my holy cows. As you get older, you just have to watch with composure when others do things differently. Whether they do things better is not the point, because anything's better than inertia. Ossification mustn't spread to the soul. Life means change.

This is also true of my work at Sant'Anselmo. When my term of office has finished or come to an end earlier due to illness or death, others will continue. I've even made provisions for such an eventuality by creating an advisory body that supports me and is privy to all the various operations. It consists of three abbots, and any of them could take my place at any time.

I would, incidentally, have been a bad student of Prior Paul if I had ever assumed the airs and graces of an autocrat. What was his recommendation? "Most Reverend Father, don't consider yourself so terribly important; don't take yourself so terribly seriously." I silently hope that I've always followed this advice.

23.

....

Postscript

It's probably my curiosity—this constant feeling that things don't have to be as they are. Even when something has become established, and has been done the same way by everyone since time immemorial, it could be done differently. But how?

"Find out," I tell myself. "Brace yourself and try something different, something new, maybe something better. And don't give up until you've figured out what it is you want to do." This has been the source of my energy, my spirit of enterprise, for nearly seventy-five years, and it doesn't dry up. This is why I'm not willing to sit back. This is why I don't wait for others but prefer to take the lead. There's still enough fuel in the tank, and the engine is still pulling strongly.

And I still look at the world wide-eyed like a child. In old age, the eyes and ears are even sharper. I now see things I overlooked in the past and hear what I used to ignore. But like a child, I can still be filled with wonder. Like a child I want to know how a story continues, and would like most of all to be a part of it.

During my studies a confrere said to me, "I'm dreading the day when I grow up." I knew what he was talking about. "Me too," I replied.

Even though I don't want to live for five hundred years, I'd still like to return to earth after five hundred years to see what's become of it. Acquiring inner tranquility doesn't mean no longer taking pleasure in the ups and downs of life. I like to intervene where societal problems or developments in the Church are involved, and I follow political developments with great interest, sometimes at a distance and sometimes up close. There are so many questions I would like answers to.

Where will the People's Republic of China stand in a few years? How will geopolitical systems change? Will we be able to prevent a clash of cultures in a world that is growing closer together? Will progress in Christian ecumenism and interreligious dialogue help make the world more peaceful?

Why should these things stop being of interest to me just because I've gotten older?

I'm not even tired of acquiring knowledge for which I might have no practical use. For example, I have no idea if I will return to Korea, but it still gives me pleasure to improve my Korean language skills.

Now and then also, I read passages of the New Testament in Swahili just so I can exchange a few words with our students from East Africa in their mother tongue. And I owe so many insights to the conversations I've had with these young students from all over the world! What would otherwise be a matter-of-fact news report in the press comes to life when I talk to people it touches—and again a window opens.

I'm also still curious about technical developments. At my age you're immune to the alleged sources of happiness emanating from Silicon Valley—but I am curious what will come in the fields of medicine, human genetics, and space research. In the half century between my philosophical and scientific studies and the contemporary era, research has progressed so rapidly that here, too, I'm repeatedly filled with wonder.

And when a vacuum-cleaner robot came on the market I was all for it—and I enjoy mine. I set my model so that it starts at a certain time and operates along fixed routes on the carpet of my study. And if it really overlooks a particular spot, all I have to do is point it there. An excellent thing.

Of course you don't have to throw everything overboard. There are things to which I have remained and shall remain true. Music being one of them. I repeatedly take out my flute, and I look forward to every performance with my friends in the rock band Feedback. When I can, I play one of my Helloween, Iron Maiden, or Rolling Stones CDs—and ask myself where the time's gone.

Yes, it's okay to cling to the past—human beings need a cultural home. As long as you don't fall into the trap of becoming a victim of your memories. *Stay flexible both mentally and physically,* I say to myself, and so on summer evenings before the "third half of the day," I swim my thirty lengths in the fourteen-meter swimming pool (to which I owe my crooked toe). Only a flexible human being can bring about change.

It often astonishes me how people much younger than I am cling to tradition, how hard it is to persuade them to go in a new direction. I feel comfortable as a pioneer of new ideas, whether mine or those of other people. Recently I've acquired a role model in this respect who is some years older than I: Pope Francis.

He has gotten rid of the Baroque tendencies in the Vatican. As well as being flexible, he is courageous—for example, publicly rebuking curia cardinals who cling to their dogmatic and canonical views when a pastoral attitude is what is needed for communicating the message of the Bible.

Not everyone likes this outsider and lateral thinker; even so-called progressive people in the Church find him difficult to deal with. And while Pope Francis is trying to bring about a change of mentality, Germany is, as usual, demanding structural reforms. As if structures are life-giving! But the man from Argentina is not trying to reinvent Christianity; he only wants to lead the Church back to the Gospel, the Good News.

———◆———

Curiosity, impartiality, courage, freedom, and frankness in thinking and talking: these can be the strengths that distinguish us in old age, in that phase of life that opens our eyes to what is essential, to what we really need. Man does not live on bread alone. . . .

The creators of Western culture, most notably monks and Enlightenment philosophers, had a passion for truth and were capable of being inspired by it. Are those people who are warning us about the Islamization of the West campaigning for our spiritual values? It doesn't look like it to me. They lack that passion for truth. We won't demonstrate away Islam—we don't need to. But you can oppose it with your own steadfast, living faith.

This requires us to be fired up with passion—a passion for truth, not the dictates of political correctness; a passion for freedom, not the growing paternalism; a passion for justice that takes everybody's character into consideration, not the prevailing ideology of equality; and a passion for love of the human race.

The philosophy of Stoicism and religions of the East preach dispassion; Jews and Christians know a God who loves passionately, and I am convinced that it won't be those who are rising up in anger who will rescue the West, but those who hold fast to this God.

I'm still responsible for Sant'Anselmo and the order. This responsibility has not only been transmitted to me by election; I've also been called to it by Jesus Christ. Passivity is therefore not in my vocabulary; I leave it to others to make things comfortable for themselves. Until the day I'm confronted with heaven—eternity—life is an open book.

ABOUT PARACLETE PRESS

Who We Are

Paraclete Press is a publisher of books, recordings, and DVDs on Christian spirituality. Our publishing represents a full expression of Christian belief and practice—from Catholic to Evangelical, from Protestant to Orthodox.

We are the publishing arm of the Community of Jesus, an ecumenical monastic community in the Benedictine tradition. As such, we are uniquely positioned in the marketplace without connection to a large corporation and with informal relationships to many branches and denominations of faith.

What We Are Doing

PARACLETE PRESS BOOKS | Paraclete publishes books that show the richness and depth of what it means to be Christian. Although Benedictine spirituality is at the heart of all that we do, we publish books that reflect the Christian experience across many cultures, time periods, and houses of worship. We publish books that nourish the vibrant life of the church and its people.

We have several different series, including the best-selling Paraclete Essentials and Paraclete Giants series of classic texts in contemporary English; Voices from the Monastery—men and women monastics writing about living a spiritual life today; award-winning poetry; best-selling gift books for children on the occasions of baptism and first communion; and the Active Prayer Series that brings creativity and liveliness to any life of prayer.

MOUNT TABOR BOOKS | Paraclete's newest series, Mount Tabor Books, focuses on the arts and literature as well as liturgical worship and spirituality, and was created in conjunction with the Mount Tabor Ecumenical Centre for Art and Spirituality in Barga, Italy.

PARACLETE RECORDINGS | From Gregorian chant to contemporary American choral works, our recordings celebrate the best of sacred choral music composed through the centuries that create a space for heaven and earth to intersect. Paraclete Recordings is the record label representing the internationally acclaimed choir Gloriæ Dei Cantores, praised for their "rapt and fathomless spiritual intensity" by American Record Guide; the Gloriæ Dei Cantores Schola, specializing in the study and performance of Gregorian chant; and the other instrumental artists of the Arts Empowering Life Foundation.

Paraclete Press is also privileged to be the exclusive North American distributor of the recordings of the Monastic Choir of St. Peter's Abbey in Solesmes, France, long considered to be a leading authority on Gregorian chant.

PARACLETE VIDEO | Our DVDs offer spiritual help, healing, and biblical guidance for a broad range of life issues including grief and loss, marriage, forgiveness, facing death, bullying, addictions, Alzheimer's, and spiritual formation.

Learn more about us at our website:
www.paracletepress.com or phone us
toll-free at 1.800.451.5006

SCAN
TO
READ
MORE

Also Available from Paraclete Press. . .

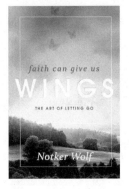

Faith Can Give Us Wings
The Art of Letting Go
Notker Wolf
978-1-61261-303-1
$15.99 Paperback

"Why do you look so happy?"
people have been asking Notker Wolf for years, now.
So he set out to answer them in this lively book. A relationship with God, he explains, can feel like falling in love, when it seems that butterflies are fluttering around in your stomach. Then, beauty, joy, belief, trust, and forgiveness are his subjects, all in an effort to show his readers how it is possible to have wings of faith—and fly!
"Notker Wolf is a gift to the monastic community, the Church and the world in Christ. This book brings out the best of his multifaceted spiritual and natural gifts. I recommend it highly."
— JOHN MICHAEL TALBOT

"This insightful book can speak to the emptiness we all experience at times and perk us up so that we take notice of what really matters. By reading and reflecting on these ideas, you might just discover the beauty and fullness a faith perspective has to offer.
You may even learn to soar!"
—SISTER JUDITH ANN HEBLE, OSB,
Moderator, Communio Internationalis Benedictinarum, Sacred Heart
Monastery, Lisle, Illinois

Available through your local bookseller or through Paraclete Press
www.paracletepress.com; 1-800-451-5006